AUDIO
FOR
AUTHORS

AUDIOBOOKS, PODCASTING,
AND VOICE TECHNOLOGIES

Joanna Penn

Audio for Authors: Audiobooks, Podcasting and Voice Technologies

Copyright © Joanna Penn (2020)

ISBN:
978-1-913321-21-5- Paperback
978-1-913321-22-2- Large Print
978-1-913321-23-9 - Hardback

Published by Curl Up Press

Requests to publish work from this book should be sent to:
joanna@TheCreativePenn.com

Cover and Interior Design: JD Smith

Printed by Lightning Source Ltd

www.CurlUpPress.com

Dedicated to my podcast audience at
The Creative Penn Podcast, and in particular,
to my patrons supporting the show on Patreon. Thank
you for your support, both emotional and financial.
You keep me going back to the mic every week!

Contents

Introduction

I remember lying in bed aged nine listening to my story tapes as the rain pattered down on the windows outside. I was cozy in my room under the blankets, but my imagination was far away in the Kingdom of Ruritania as the story of *The Prisoner of Zenda* played on. Until, of course, I had to turn the tape over!

I also loved Prokofiev's *Peter and the Wolf* — I can still hear the music — but my local library had a tiny selection of tapes, so I had to listen to the same stories over and over again.

Books on tape were limited by the cost of production — studios, audio equipment, sound engineers, narrators, physical production — as well as the format itself, which meant that books were often abridged to fit into boxes. They had to be physically packaged, shipped, stored, and shelved, so the market was limited.

But now, those limitations are gone.

The cost of production and distribution has come down dramatically. Audio equipment is a lot cheaper than it once was, and you can record in a home studio or hire a professional narrator and producer for a reasonable rate.

Smartphones and streaming audio in cars and homes mean that the physical distribution of audiobooks is no longer necessary, and the rise of podcasts has led to more people consuming audio. Length is no longer a problem, and there are ever-expanding opportunities for global distribution. Libraries don't need to physically stock boxes of tapes anymore. They can have unlimited audio in their catalogs and even use pricing like the pay-per-checkout model, which is great for authors and also fantastic for readers, and those kids — like me in the 80s — who love listening to stories.

We are part of a renaissance in audio creativity and consumption, and it's an exciting time to be in the market!

Who am I?

I'm Joanna Penn, non-fiction author and award-nominated thriller writer under J.F.Penn, international speaker and award-winning creative entrepreneur. I started *The Creative Penn Podcast* in 2009. At the time of writing, it has been downloaded over four million times across 222 countries. I licensed my first audiobooks in 2013 and started recording my own non-fiction in 2015. In 2019, I started a second podcast, *Books and Travel*. I've edited and produced my own audio and also worked with professional freelancers. I've been a host and a guest on hundreds of shows, and as an avid reader, I listen to podcasts and audiobooks almost every day. Yes, I'm an audio junkie, and in this book, I'll show you the possibilities ahead.

Part 1 discusses audiobooks and everything you need to write and adapt your writing for audio, work with professional narrators or self-narrate, license your rights or independently publish your audiobook, and tips for marketing.

Part 2 delves into the world of podcasting and why it's such a great medium for authors, how to pitch and be a fantastic guest, as well as how to start your own show if that's your goal.

Part 3 covers voice technologies, including dictation and voice-led writing, voice assistants, smart speakers, optimizing for voice search, and a glimpse of a possible future where artificial intelligence enhances what is possible for audio creators and publishers.

Chapter notes, references and resources are included in the Appendices and on the download page at:

TheCreativePenn.com/audiobookdownload

I hope you find this book useful on your journey into audio creativity.

> Note: There are affiliate links within this book to products and services that I recommend and use personally. This means that I receive a small percentage of sales at no extra cost to you, and in some cases, you may receive a discount for using my links. I only recommend products and services that I believe are great for authors, so I hope you find them useful.

Why audio? Why now?

The advent of mobile and streaming internet speeds alongside cheap technology for creation and consumption have exploded the potential for audio in the last decade, and it just keeps getting better. Here are some recent headlines:

- The Audio Publishers Association reports seven years of double-digit revenue growth for audiobooks in the USA.

- *The Independent* reports that audiobook sales are predicted to overtake ebook sales in the UK in 2020.

- Tom Webster, Senior Vice President at Edison Research noted, "This is a watershed moment for podcasting — a true milestone. With over half of Americans 12+ saying that they have listened to a podcast, the medium has firmly crossed into the mainstream."

- According to the Edison Infinite Dial Report, "time spent listening to online audio reached a record high in 2019, with weekly online audio listeners reporting an average of nearly 17 hours of listening in the last week."

There is clearly a growing demand for audio in all kinds of formats, and as creators, we are well placed to take advantage of this shift in consumer behavior.

Audiobooks are the fastest-growing segment of the publishing market, and more opportunities arise every month for authors who want to get their books into the format. We can license our audiobook rights, work with professional narrators, or learn how to narrate our own work, distributing audiobooks through an ever-growing network of mobile applications to increase revenue.

We can start a podcast or appear as an interview guest on other people's shows to reach readers directly and spread the word about our books. We can build trust and a more intimate relationship with listeners by using our voices, which are far more personal than words on a page.

Audio will help you stand out

"We're moving inexorably toward a subscription-driven, human-driven, emotion-driven, ad-free, funnel-free, big brand loyalty-free world."

Mark W Schaefer, Marketing Rebellion

The written word is an increasingly crowded marketplace. There are more books published every day alongside many thousands of articles and many millions of social media updates.

At the same time, people are listening to more podcasts and audiobooks, making time for consumption in their busy lives while doing other things.

If your book is available in audio, you can potentially reach these readers with your words, and even your spoken voice if you self-narrate. The audiobook space is nowhere near as crowded as the market for ebooks or print, because the cost of entry is still much higher than converting text to a digital file.

An author who performs well is memorable — whether that is live at an event or on a podcast interview about their book. But good performance takes practice, and many authors prefer to create alone, and stay away from book marketing. I understand that feeling, but if you want to reach readers and sell books, you need to step outside your comfort zone and meet people where they are.

If you build a connection with readers, you will sell more books, because voice fosters a relationship. Listeners feel like they know you, like you and trust you, and that is an authentic way to stand out in a noisy world.

This book is intended to push you out of your comfort zone, because the world is changing, and there are more ways to reach readers through audio than ever before. The time is now for embracing audio, so I hope you will join me on the journey.

The audio-first ecosystem

This book includes different kinds of audio because it's not just about one finished product — the audiobook. It's more about an ecosystem of audio that suits a particular type of consumer. Here's an example.

A typical day in my household

I make breakfast while listening to a news briefing, a micro-podcast of around eight minutes, on my phone. As I'm about to walk to my writing café, I ask Siri on my Apple Watch, "What's the weather like today?" so I can decide on what coat to wear and whether to take an umbrella.

I listen to a podcast on my 20-minute walk to the writing café and either continue the podcast on the way back or listen to some of an audiobook. While listening to a podcast interview, the author mentions their book, so I add it to my Wish List on the Audible app, or my To Do list if it's not in audio format. I used to read non-fiction in ebook format, but now I listen to audiobooks and buy the print edition as well if I want to take notes. I like to learn fast, so I listen to both audiobooks and podcasts at 1.25 or 1.5x speed. Normal speed is just too slow for me now.

My husband works in his office in the loft and uses an Apple HomePod to listen to music or play podcasts during his workday. He also uses it to call his mum in New Zealand.

One of us will prepare dinner while listening to an audio-book or podcast, and the other one will clear up while doing the same.

In bed before sleeping, I read fiction on my Kindle, but my husband listens to a fantasy audiobook to relax. He loves the long epic fantasy audiobooks of 30+ hours and will consume huge series for weeks at a time.

Other common daily situations

Our household is child-free and car-free by choice, but of course, there are many other times when people want to listen to audio. The Audio Publishers Association reported at Frankfurt Book Fair 2019 that most US audiobook listeners consume audiobooks while driving, at home, traveling, and exercising, while some also listened at work.

A commuter drives for 45 minutes each way every weekday and listens to podcasts and audiobooks, or uses Spotify to recommend a drive-time mix of personalized audio content. Google Auto, Apple Carplay, and Amazon Alexa make it easy to stream audio in cars.

Whispersync technology means that you can be reading on your phone or device at breakfast, then get in your car and continue listening where you stopped reading, and when you get home, cook dinner while listening again, all without losing your place.

A child comes home from school and asks a smart speaker in the home to read a story or play a favorite song. They no longer have to bug mum or dad to read to them or find the song on their phone. They can just ask the smart speaker.

Parents are also happier for children to interact with an audio-first device, as it means less screen time.

An older person at home alone all day asks their voice assistant to play their favorite radio station or call their daughter for a chat.

A library user logs into the local website, checks out a digital audiobook from the comfort of home, and starts listening straight away.

You are not necessarily your market

Your goal is to have your books available to those who choose an audio-first ecosystem even if you don't behave this way yourself.

Consider how an audio-first consumer might come upon your work. I mainly discover non-fiction books through podcasts, and I prefer to buy them in audio format. If you have a non-fiction book that might be relevant to me, I am unlikely to discover it unless you have some kind of audio presence. You are virtually invisible to me as a consumer. If you write huge fantasy series and your books are not in audio, you are missing out on a dedicated reader like my husband. We are just two people in a growing audio-first market, so who are you failing to reach?

Think wide distribution.
Think global, digital, and mobile

It's important to remember that audiobooks are not just about Audible, and podcasting is not just about Apple Podcasts. The digital audio ecosystem might have started in the US, but these days, it is much wider, and things are changing all the time.

Listeners can choose to consume audiobooks through sites like Storytel, Kobo Audio, Scribd or Google Play as well as checking them out through library systems like Hoopla or OverDrive. Listeners in Africa can choose Streetlib or Publiseer, and there are many more emerging options.

In terms of podcasting, listeners in the US overwhelmingly use Apple Podcasts, whereas Spotify is the leading podcast platform in Germany. Google Podcasts are now available as the default on Android devices, which make up 78% of the global mobile market share, according to Libsyn data presented at Podcast Movement 2019.

Some listeners even prefer YouTube for audio-only content, since many use the platform for music, and it makes sense to prefer a specific platform as it learns your preferences over time.

The audio ecosystem is global, so make sure your work is available everywhere.

Sell more books through an audio-first ecosystem

We are authors. We want to sell more books and reach more readers with our stories and ideas. We also want to make more income. Considering the audio-first environment will help you with these goals because it's not just about having one audiobook or appearing on one podcast episode. It truly is an ecosystem that builds over time.

You need to have multiple audiobooks available so people can buy, borrow, or download as part of their subscription. You can use samples of your audio on social media as well as embedded in your website with shareable images alongside links to your audiobooks.

Maybe you have your own podcast, or at least you appear on other shows to talk about your expertise or your story. When someone asks where they can find you and your books, your call to action includes an audio option because a listener always wants more audio.

Widen your perspective to include the audio-first consumer and consider how you might reach the fastest-growing segment in publishing as it continues to grow in the coming years.

Questions:

- What is your audio behavior like right now? How has it changed over time?

- What are some examples of the audio ecosystem that you have experienced yourself or noticed in others? What devices do people use around you? What situations do people listen in?

- How can you widen your perspective to include a global, digital, audio-first consumer?

The audio mindset

In this chapter, I address some of the resistance that authors have toward audio and explore how you can shift your mindset and embrace the opportunities ahead.

"Audio is too technical."

You don't have to create audio yourself. You can appear as a guest on a podcast, and all you need is an internet connection as the host will do the recording, edits, and production. A separate microphone and headset will make the audio quality better, but you can get started without them.

You can also use an app on your phone to create audio. Most come with some kind of native recorder, but there are also lots of other options you can play with. Just press record and speak. This is a great way to practice, as you can delete the file, and no one will ever hear it.

If you want to create audio yourself, you can learn the skills over time. You learned how to do everything else in your life, so why not audio? You can also hire professional narrators, sound engineers, and others who know how to create audio, so the level of technicality is really up to you. Start with the basics and improve over time.

"Audio is too expensive."

It can be as expensive as you want it to be. Some people geek out on technical equipment, but as above, you can podcast with just an internet connection and a phone. You don't have to invest in a microphone, a home sound booth, or specific software. All that can come later if you need it and even then, I've used the same microphone for years, and it was less than $100. I also started out using free audio software, Audacity.

In terms of audiobooks, if you're not narrating them yourself, you can do royalty-split deals where you pay nothing upfront and share royalties with the narrator over time instead.

Investment in audio certainly takes time, but it doesn't need to cost a lot of money.

"I'm introverted, shy, or have social anxiety."

Introversion, shyness, and social anxiety are not the same things, but I group them here as they form a kind of spectrum.

I'm an introvert, defined as someone who gets energy from being alone and finds interaction with others tiring. I am not shy, but sometimes I think I have a form of social anxiety as I struggle with large groups and will often leave if I feel overwhelmed.

As an introvert, I love podcasting because it's usually just a one-on-one conversation with another professional, and I am alone in my home office when it happens. I don't have to go anywhere or see anyone. When narrating my own audiobooks, I'm alone in my sound booth, so both situations are perfect for introvert creators.

If you're shy or have social anxiety, you may still find the idea of an online conversation difficult. You have to decide whether it's worth addressing your fears and stepping outside your comfort zone in order to achieve your goals. I still have heart palpitations before interviews and often have to do some breathing exercises to calm my nerves, but it's definitely worth it.

"Audio takes time away from my 'real' creative work."

At the time of writing, *The Creative Penn Podcast* has been downloaded over four million times by listeners in 222 countries.

I have sold books in 136 countries and have certainly sold fewer than four million copies, so my podcast has reached more people than my books. I get emails every day from listeners who say that the show has changed their lives and helped them release their books into the world, so it clearly has an impact.

I may have started my show as a way to learn, meet other authors and market my books, but it has turned into an essential part of my creative body of work — just as important as my non-fiction books, perhaps even more so.

Every show starts with the written word, and for my solo episodes, I create specifically for audio-first. I am even writing a travel memoir through podcast episodes on *Books and Travel*.

The process of editing for audio narration has helped me become a better writer and improved my creative work. You have to think about language, sound, and how words will land on the ear of the listener. You have to expand your vocabulary to avoid repetition. You have to structure the flow of the book carefully, and much more, as covered in chapter 1.2. You can also create straight for audio specifically by writing scripts, audio originals, podcast fiction, or narrative non-fiction. There is no limit to creative possibility, and audio is just another medium to consider.

"I hate my voice."

This is one of the most common reasons that authors don't want to get into audio, so I'm going to be blunt.

It doesn't matter what you think.

It's not about you. It's about the listener.

They are the ones who get to judge — and they *will* judge. Some people will turn off because they don't connect with your voice, but others will carry on listening because they enjoy it.

Take comfort in the fact that you cannot even hear your voice in the same way as other people do. When you speak, your vocal cords set off sound waves that vibrate inside your skull, whereas other people hear the sound externally. Of course, you can listen to a recording, but you will still hear it differently to other people because you have already pre-judged yourself.

Get over it!

Learn to love what you have and make the most of your voice.

Of course, you can get voice coaching if you want to improve, but it's worth giving it a go first because, in all likelihood, you are judging yourself too harshly.

"I have a distinctive accent."

We all have accents because we all come from different places, but usually when someone thinks this way, there are two different possibilities. The first is a native English speaker with a distinctive tone, for example, Scottish or Australian.

The other kind is when the speaker has English as a second language. There is a distinctive accent because of where they come from originally. Even if someone is fluent in English, there will still be an accent.

Both of these have benefits, as they can make you stand out from the crowd when narrating your own work or as a guest or host on podcasts. Those who enjoy your accent will love it. Those who don't will just turn off.

In the past, the BBC in the UK would only allow Received Pronunciation (RP), commonly known as the Queen's English, on its programs. But in recent years, even the BBC has embraced regional accents, and now it's more likely that you will hear diverse voices on the radio and TV than RP. So, if you have any kind of accent, you are in good company.

If you are worried that you can't be understood, record yourself and ask some of your target audience to comment.

Again, you can get voice coaching, but if your target market enjoys your voice, then it shouldn't be a problem.

"I don't listen to audiobooks or podcasts, so why would I bother creating them?"

Since you're reading this book, I presume you're in some way convinced that you need to think about audio as an author in terms of selling more books and reaching more readers. I would also suggest that you start listening to some, even just to test out the various options and see what people are creating out there. It might give you some great ideas!

Questions:

- What is stopping you from doing audio?

- How can you shift your mindset to embrace the possibilities of the audio ecosystem?

Part 1: Audiobooks

1.1 Types of audiobooks

There are different types of audiobooks and various reasons for people to listen to them. This is important to understand, so you don't compare your book to another that might serve a different niche. The audio ecosystem is broad, and your work will fit somewhere.

Here are some of the different types of audiobooks.

(1) Books read by a famous actor or voice talent

If the narrator is Stephen Fry or Miriam Margolyes, then you might buy the book for the pleasure of their performance regardless of the content. There might also be a voice talent in your niche that you love listening to, and many narrators have fans who buy books just to hear them speak.

(2) Books read by the author — they might be famous, they might not be!

Some audiobooks are naturally better when read by the author, for example, famous memoirs like *Who Am I, Again?* by Lenny Henry or *Born a Crime* by Trevor Noah, both of whom use accents to portray their history and bring a richness that no third-party narrator could ever deliver. This category also includes humorous books by stand-up comedians and personal non-fiction where the author has an existing audience through a podcast or TV show.

I love listening to audiobooks read by the author, even if they have some imperfections. Thriller author Scott Sigler's rendition of *Infected*, Stephen King's *On Writing*, *Women who Run with the Wolves* by Clarissa Pinkola Estes, and *Big Magic* by Elizabeth Gilbert are just some examples.

Some authors will do different accents for characters, and others will do a straight read. Both can work well. Distinctive accents and under-represented voices are also important in this niche.

(3) Full-cast production audio with sound effects

This is immersive entertainment and expensive to produce, but it can be spectacular if done well. BBC Radio Drama has been a world leader in this niche for many years, and now internet first companies have added to the content available. Audible Originals has a number of these productions, including *War of the Worlds*, *Alien: Sea of Sorrows*, and Jane Austen's *Emma*.

There are also serial audiobook productions that are more like podcasts in that you download episodes per story, for example, *Six Degrees of Assassination*, a 10-part audio drama by MJ Arlidge.

(4) Audio for information, entertainment, or inspiration — as long as the narrator is bearable, it's all good!

Recently, I had lunch with a friend of mine from university. She's a working mum with young kids who spends a lot of time in her car or on the train, and she's always busy at home. She loves to read, but if a book is not in audio, she won't even consider it. She only has time to read while doing other things.

She is studying for a degree and wants her textbooks and academic journals in audio. She would be happy to listen to books in an AI voice as she cares about the content, not the narrator in this context.

I have the same attitude for much of my listening, and I often use 1.5x speed to consume books faster. I find 'normal' narration speed too slow in general, but I will change the setting for books with beautiful language or performance poetry, for example, *Underland* by Robert Macfarlane or *Brand New Ancients* by Kate Tempest.

* * *

Audiobooks differ in terms of their production type, but also in when and why someone might listen. For example, I listen to non-fiction audio for information when I'm walking, doing chores, or exercising. I also enjoy full-cast audio drama when I'm tired and want entertainment but no more screen time. Understanding the different types of audiobook will help you decide where yours might fit and also to be aware of the opportunities available for audio creation.

Questions:

- What are the different types of audiobook?

- Where might your work fit into the ecosystem?

- Go to your preferred audiobook store online and sample some of the different types of audiobooks to see what you enjoy. You can sample for free, so it's worth trying a broad range.

1.2 Writing, adapting and editing for audio

"When you're editing, think of your book as a script for performance. Practice reading it aloud – it'll help you pick up edits to improve the clarity and flow."

Jules Horne, Writing for Audiobooks:
Audio First for Flow and Impact

Some books are more suited to audio than others. Some can be performed with no adaptation at all, whereas others will need to be adapted specifically for the format.

If your book is narrative with mostly text, then it will likely be fine for a straight read. But if it's a scientific textbook full of diagrams and tables, or designed for a specific physical layout, like a graphic novel, then it will need adaptation.

Adapting and editing your work for audio can improve your writing

An audiobook has two voices — the voice of the writer from the text and the voice of the narrator. Both have to be resonant, but even a fantastic narrator can't make a poorly written book sound good, so you need to write in a way that enables a great performance.

If you have licensed your book for audio, you won't be able to update the text. It will be performed as is. But if you're an independent author, you can edit your existing work for audio, or you can use these tips to edit before publication to ensure your audiobook is a great experience.

One of my favorite audiobooks is *Underland* by Robert MacFarlane, narrated by Roy McMillan. It's narrative non-fiction, but the writing is almost poetic in its resonance. It makes me want to become a better writer so I can produce something as beautiful. This is why writing for audio is exciting — because it makes us better at the craft, and that can only be a good thing!

Of course, not all writing should be poetic or literary, and my own thrillers are fast-paced and plot-driven, but it's an example of what is possible.

Start by reading a chapter or two out loud and listen to how it sounds

Writing for the ear is different from writing for the eyes and calls for different skills. Words on the page don't stand out as much as those read aloud. You can use text-to-speech software like Natural Reader if you don't want to read it yourself, but you need to train your ear to listen for what works and what doesn't.

Don't confuse the reader

The listening experience is linear, so you need to ensure you keep forward movement without confusing the listener. Of course, chapters can be wound back, but many listeners will be in the middle of something else like driving, cooking, or exercising, so most will just continue on. If you lose the thread of forward motion for too long, the listener may turn off altogether.

Watch out for repeated sounds

The editorial process will usually catch repeated written words but similar sounding words can hit the same audio note in narration. You might not have noticed them in the text as they are spelled differently. For example, the words *you, blue, tattoo,* and *interview* all start and end with different letters. They look different on the page, but they strike the same note when read aloud.

In the same way, repetition can work if you have a point to make, but sometimes it can be jarring to the listener if it is done too much.

Break up long sentences with multiple sub-clauses

These may be difficult for the narrator — as they have to breathe somewhere — and also hard to follow for the reader. Consider splitting into shorter sentences or adding commas where appropriate.

Back matter

Appendices, Acknowledgements and other back matter are not read as part of the audiobook, so if there is something you specifically want included, then make sure it is in the body of the manuscript. This is why I've included the references for this book in an Appendix rather than at the end of each chapter.

Specific issues with fiction

A classic recommendation for writing dialogue in fiction is to use 'said' with a character name rather than other words like 'uttered' or 'pronounced.' This is because 'said' almost disappears for a reader on the page and is scarcely noticed, although its meaning is understood.

However, with audio, the **repetition of a word is highly noticeable** and repeated sounds can dominate a passage. Rewrite with synonyms for 'said,' or use action to make it clear who the speaker is without resorting to dialogue tags.

Contractions — or the lack of them — can also become more obvious in audio. For example, "I am not going to the park," might be spoken as "I'm not going to the park." When we type dialogue, it might be more formal than the way someone speaks or narrates.

Accents can be an issue with fiction narration. There are plenty of narrators who do a 'straight read,' but if there are accents within dialogue, you need to make it very clear where the character comes from. Make sure the narrator knows about the accent upfront, otherwise they may make choices you don't like in the finished audio.

For example, a friend of mine had an Irish character in her novel, who spoke (in her mind) with a soft brogue, but the final audiobook had the character speaking more like a comedy leprechaun. It didn't suit the somber style of the crime novel, but it was too late.

Don't confuse the reader. If you have a lot of characters appearing in a chapter with no clear character tags, you might lose the listener in the detail. With a novel on the page or screen, you can quickly flick back and see that

George was the butler and Angus was the dog, but with audio, you need to keep the forward motion. Make sure it's clear who is who, and you may have to remind listeners occasionally by adding character tags later, for example, *Angus ran alongside the canal* could become *Angus, the golden cocker spaniel, ran alongside the canal.*

"Avoid anything that diverts the listener's attention."

Jessica Kaye, The Guide to Publishing Audiobooks

Specific issues with non-fiction

Is your book straight text, or does it include images, tables, diagrams, or other elements that bring additional meaning to the material? How important are those visual elements to the book?

You can include a **PDF of downloadable material** with your audiobook that will appear on the device, or use a call to action for the listener to download extra content from your website. Still, they are unlikely to be looking at the images while listening. You may need to rewrite passages that specifically refer to diagrams. For example, *In Figure 9 above, the red line crosses the blue line at point X.* This is meaningless to a listener so either omit it in the audiobook altogether or rewrite the sentence without reference to the diagram, so the meaning is clear.

Bullet points are common in non-fiction, and although they can sometimes work, the reader might lose track if the bulleted sections are long and don't refer back to the original point. I often turn bullet-point lists into paragraphs with sub-heads for ease of narration.

Long lists of numbers are also difficult to process with audio, so rewrite those passages or omit them altogether.

Lists, in general, are hard to manage for a listener, so you might have to restructure things you take for granted in ebook or print formats. For example, I have collected all the resources for this book into an Appendix instead of listing them at the end of each chapter. This means that I can read it as a straight audiobook edition to match the ebook, enabling Whispersync on Audible and making it unabridged, but the extra information is still available if you want it.

Many non-fiction books will want to refer to other books and useful websites, but **links are hard to read aloud** with hyphens and other punctuation that no one will remember later anyway. The listener cannot click on a link via audio, so you need to rewrite the material. Use a link shortening site like Bitly or a plugin like Pretty Links for WordPress, which helps you make easy-to-read links, or you can include an Appendix with a resource list for download later. If you do include links, skip the www or http as that is unnecessary.

I always include a **download page** for each non-fiction book. I want to make the extra material available, but I also want listeners to visit my site and maybe sign up for my podcast or my newsletter list or browse more of my books.

A separate download is also useful for non-fiction as many links go dead, and sources change over time. If you have a downloadable list, you can update the material more easily than updating the original book.

You can find the download page for this audiobook at: TheCreativePenn.com/audiobookdownload

Opening and closing credits

All the platforms require opening and closing credits as part of the audiobook. There is a standard for these, although you can have small variations. Remember that people are listening, so don't use long links.

Here are the opening credits for this book.

* * *

Audio for Authors:
Audiobooks, Podcasting, and Voice Technologies

Written and narrated by Joanna Penn

Mastered by Dan Van Werkhoven

You can download the extra material
with links and further resources at:
TheCreativePenn.com/audiobookdownload

* * *

Here are the closing credits. Note that you have to say, The End. I have forgotten this before, and your audiobook will be rejected if you don't include it, so I have added it to my closing credit template.

* * *

THE END

This has been *Audio for Authors:*
Audiobooks, Podcasting, and Voice Technologies.

Written and narrated by Joanna Penn

Mastered by Dan Van Werkhoven

You can download the extra material
with links and further resources at:
TheCreativePenn.com/audiobookdownload

You can find more audiobooks, my free weekly podcast
for writers, and more resources at TheCreativePenn.com

* * *

Writing for audio-first

This book focuses on turning existing written work into audio format, but there are more opportunities available now for writing audio-first material. If you have a stage play or a screenplay, you could turn that into a performance piece for an audio original to go out on radio or podcasts or license it to audio-focused subscription services like Audible.

Ultimately, audio is a different medium, but the knowledge that our words will be spoken may start to change the way we write in the first place.

Questions:

- How much adaptation will your book need for audio?

- Why is editing and adapting your work a good idea?

- What are some of the things to consider specifically for fiction?

- What are some of the things to consider specifically for non-fiction?

- What are the possibilities for audio-first writing?

1.3 Intellectual property considerations for audiobooks

Note: I am not a lawyer, and this is not legal advice, purely my opinion, based on experience. Please consult a legal professional for your situation.

Copyright

Your original work is automatically protected by copyright as soon as your ideas are in a fixed form, like a manuscript, a finished book, or an audiobook. Copyright covers the text but also the sound recording and anything created from those works.

You don't need to register copyright for it to be applied to your work, but if you do register it and later need to sue someone for infringement, you may be entitled to more in terms of damages, so it can be worth registering in certain jurisdictions.

In traditional publishing, the print book distributed through physical bookstores has traditionally been the primary format. The ebook has now been absorbed into that primary sale, but audiobooks are still, almost universally, treated as a subsidiary right.

Have you signed a contract with a publisher for your book?

There are different kinds of audiobook rights, and as with any licensing agreement, you can make them very specific. For example, 'single narrator audiobook in English for UK/Commonwealth for retail and library markets,' is very different to 'all audio rights for any production format worldwide in every language.'

If you have signed anything regarding your book, check the contract to see what rights you have licensed.

There might be a clause like the following: "You license all formats existing and to be created in all languages and in all territories for the life of copyright." If you have signed this, then you do not hold the rights to your audiobook, or in fact, any rights at all.

There may be a reversion clause later in the contract, and you might be able to get the rights back if the publisher has not produced the audiobook within a specific time period. In this case, speak to your agent or publisher about getting your audio rights back.

If the clause is more specific, and especially if it is an older contract, you might have more options. For example, the audio rights might cover tapes or CDs rather than digital format, or the US/Canada territory and not worldwide, or English only and not other languages. This gives you scope to produce audio yourself in other ways.

If you are negotiating a publishing contract, ensure you are as specific as possible with the rights you grant the publisher. If possible, term-limit them; for example, the rights revert in seven years.

There is an example Audiobook Publication Contract in *The Guide to Publishing Audiobooks* by Jessica Kaye.

Other copyright aspects to consider

Cover

Your audiobook cover should echo your other formats, but if you've licensed those to publishers, then the rights to the cover may need to be established.

If you're an independent author, you should have a contract with your book cover designer that assigns the rights for the cover to you, or licenses it exclusively. Check with your designer about the rights for the audiobook cover and have a different one made if you cannot get the correct permissions.

Recording and production

Even if you control the copyright to the underlying written work, there are also rights to the audio masters which need assigning by contract.

If you need convincing on the importance of assignment of rights, read about Taylor Swift's battle with the company that owns her original recording masters. It demonstrates the importance of who controls copyright for audio.

There is an example Copyright Assignment Contract in *The Guide to Publishing Audiobooks* by Jessica Kaye.

What about piracy for audio?

Piracy happens and will continue to happen. Of course, digital files make it easier for pirates to load audiobooks onto sites as well as ebooks. But audiobook listeners tend to listen in apps they love to use, and I choose to spend my time focusing on those listeners who are happy to pay for their books. If I come across instances of piracy, then I issue a take-down notice, but I don't actively spend my time chasing pirates.

Questions:

- Do you own the subsidiary rights for your book? If you have signed a publishing deal, did that contract include audiobook rights? For which territories and in what format?

- Has the publisher exploited those rights and produced an audiobook or are they just sitting on those rights, in which case you might be able to get them back?

- Do you have a contract with your book cover designer that also includes the audiobook cover? Do you have the rights to use a similar design? Have you ensured your contracts cover the copyright for your book cover designs?

- Do you have a contract with your audiobook narrator and/or producer? Have you been assigned the copyright for the production files?

1.4 Your options for audiobook publishing and distribution

There are several options for creating, publishing, and distributing your audiobook. This is just an overview with more detail covered in later chapters if you choose the independent route.

(1) License your audiobook rights

If you're traditionally published, chances are that your contract already includes audiobook rights. It's well worth checking because if you haven't licensed them already, you can produce the audiobook yourself or license the rights separately to the print and ebook formats.

If you're independently publishing your ebook and print books, you might still want to license your audiobook rights. For example, Andy Weir, self-published author of *The Martian*, licensed his audio to Podium Publishing. It went on to win multiple audio awards and got picked up for a major publishing deal before being made into the film starring Matt Damon.

If you want to license your rights, look at companies with a proven audio track record to pitch with your book. Check out the Audie Awards and the Audio Publishers Association, which lists some of the best companies and narrators as well as other audio professionals.

If you license your rights, you may get some input into how the project is created and distributed, or it might be out of your hands completely. Make sure there is a term limit on the deal, for example, seven years, so you know when you will get your rights back, especially if the audio has not been produced.

If you want to license your audio rights, I recommend *The Guide to Publishing Audiobooks* by Jessica Kaye, which goes into licensing from the publisher perspective and includes template contracts, so you know what to watch out for.

(2) Hire a professional narrator for your book and publish it independently

If you listen to a lot of audiobooks, you might have a narrator in mind already. You can always email and ask if they are available. If you don't know who you want, you can work with a company that will help you find the right narrator and then choose from auditions. You can pay a narrator outright or potentially do a royalty-split deal over a specific number of years.

(3) Narrate the book yourself and publish it independently

Many non-fiction authors, and some fiction authors, choose to narrate their own work, especially if they have a speaking platform, podcast, or other business where they are well-known.

There are many different companies that help authors create and distribute audiobooks. Personally, I use ACX and Findaway Voices, so I will focus on these in the upcoming chapters.

Questions:

- If you want to license your audio rights, do you have proven sales or a reason that a publisher might want those rights?

1.5 How to find and work with a professional narrator

If you have licensed your audiobook rights, your publisher will choose the narrator. They may ask your opinion, but they may not, so if you want to be consulted, put that into the contract. Some authors only hear their audiobook once it is up for sale. Some are happy, others not so much. But if you license your rights, you have no choice.

If you independently publish, you can choose your narrator, and there are a few ways to go about this.

If you regularly listen to audiobooks and you have a narrator in mind, go to their website and check out their rates. If they're popular, you might not be able to book them anyway, or they might be too expensive, but you can always ask.

If you don't listen to audiobooks, it can be challenging to find the right voice for your book. As authors, the voice in our heads sounds a certain way, but that might not be the right voice for the narration, so try to be open to the process, and you will discover what works along the way.

Narrators specialize in different things, so you'll need to listen to a number of them before you decide. Some may be trained performers with an acting background, others might be radio professionals with a presenting background. Some simply have a voice that resonates with you or one that's the right tone and demographic for your book.

There are also different reading and performance styles, for example, a multi-character specialist or a more immersive storyteller, or something in between. Think of it as a casting decision and bear your genre in mind when choosing. Once the narrator's voice is attached to your book, you will be linked together for years to come, so it's essential to find the right one.

Findaway Voices can help you find the right narrator for your book. Once you upload the manuscript, they determine possibilities, and you work through a shortlist of samples to find someone appropriate.

If you use ACX, upload your manuscript, add notes about sales or your platform, and initial preference on voice, for example, US adult male, and then narrators will submit auditions. You can also reach out to narrators on the platform or directly through their websites to solicit auditions. If you are a new author with no platform or proven sales, you might only get auditions from new narrators looking for experience. It's your choice at that point whether to give someone new a go since you are both just starting out or to work with an established narrator.

You can also find narrators through your author contacts and go looking for them instead of passively waiting for auditions. I actively found two of my narrators through recommendations from friends, and another found me through ACX.

Once you find a narrator, listen to their audition and email them with any questions. For example, "In the sample, you did a great rendition of my main male character, but how would you narrate his daughter's voice?"

Contracts

There are two main types of contracts with narrators:

(1) Per finished hour rate calculated on how long the audiobook will be. It's usually about 9,000 words per finished hour, so a 70,000-word book would be around eight hours. Rates typically vary between US$200-US$500 per finished hour, depending on the narrator's experience. You might pay a deposit or just pay on completion.

Once the audiobook is complete and on sale, any income flows only to you. You do not need to pay the narrator any more money.

Most authors with decent sales in other formats cover these upfront costs within the first year, and future sales will be profit. If you retain the rights, then this can be a significant income stream over the long term.

(2) Royalty share deal based on the number of years in the contract. For example, if you sign an exclusive deal with a narrator on ACX, you pay nothing upfront, and the narrator gets a 50% royalty share for seven years.

Voices Share through Findaway Voices works slightly differently in that the author pays half the cost of a normal audiobook, and the narrator gets a 20% royalty. You can also buy the narrator out if you want to keep the whole royalty share later.

The contract should have an agreed timeline, for example, a date for the first chapter so you can check any initial issues and then a date for the completed audiobook.

There is an example Narration Agreement Contract in *The Guide to Publishing Audiobooks* by Jessica Kaye.

How to work successfully with a narrator

Once you've chosen a narrator and agreed on the contract, you need to provide the final manuscript for narration, usually in MSWord, ePub, or PDF format. Make sure the narrator has it in whatever format works best for them.

Make sure to listen carefully to the sample and inform the narrator of anything pertinent about the manuscript in advance. For example, "The character of Sajid is third-generation British Indian, so he speaks with a standard British accent."

The narrator will start recording and may provide an initial chapter for you to check before proceeding with the recording process. You will receive the files when they are ready for checking before publication.

Narrators are professionals. Trust them to do their job.

Once you have sent the manuscript, the narrator will prepare your book for the recording process and research pronunciation as necessary. There is an element of trust at this stage. You need to keep in mind that this is an adaptation by a professional. It is unlikely to sound exactly like the version of the book in your head, and that's OK!

I've heard horror stories from both sides of the audiobook process — authors who have been over-critical and perfectionist, insisting that they are right with pronunciation and on the flip side, narrators who haven't listened to the author's perspective at all.

Communication is critical, and the narrator will want to hear your thoughts on any specific parts of the book that need particular treatment. But you are both professionals, and you are working together on a new version of the book, so mutual respect is essential.

QA (quality assurance) or QC (quality control)

The audiobook chapters need to go through quality control, and inevitably, there will be some issues that require editing or even re-recording. This is a normal part of the process.

Many authors quality check their own audiobooks. I generally do my own as I like to listen to the book again, but you can also hire a virtual assistant to do it for you.

Listen to the complete audiobook while following the words on the manuscript to check it's correct. Note down any issues with the chapter and time stamp. For example, here are some of my notes for my narrator on one of my ARKANE thrillers with chapter number and time stamps:

Chapter 9 - 1 minute 10 - frieze - should be pronounced freeze, rather than 'frisée'

Chapter 22 - 8 minutes 52 - chamois - pronounced 'shamee' when it's a cloth, rather than 'sham-wah'

I will often include links to pronunciation videos to back up my interpretation.

There might also be pauses that are too long or too short, as well as repeated phrases where the edit was missed, or extraneous sounds that need to be removed. Note those down, too.

If there is a consistent mispronunciation across the whole book, you need to decide whether it's worth asking for retakes, or whether you can just leave it. Most listeners won't know the difference anyway, and even if they do notice, most will ignore it as we all skip over the occasional typo in a print or ebook.

For my ARKANE series, my wonderful narrator, Veronica Giguere, is American, and my characters are international. Sometimes, I have to correct a British word that needs to be pronounced correctly. For example, Magdalen College, Oxford, is pronounced Maud-lin, not Mag-da-len as it is spelled. But there are other words that I won't correct, for example, 'shone' is pronounced differently by Americans than British people, but I leave that as spoken.

Editing is a difficult and time-consuming business, and making changes to an audiobook is much more compli-cated than updates to a print or ebook edition. Remember, this is an adaptation, so unless something is a clear error, it might be best to let it go.

If there are a lot of issues that need fixing in every chapter, then there are two possible reasons: The narrator is not doing their job properly, or you are too stringent with your quality check.

Finished files

After QA, editing, and mastering, the narrator will provide the finished audio files per chapter. These should match the correct technical specifications, and if they fail the valida-tion process, the narrator should fix and provide new files. They may work with a producer and sound engineer or do it themselves, but whatever their arrangement, the narrator is responsible for providing the correct files. They may load them into ACX or Findaway, or they may be shared in a dropbox folder so you can access and upload them yourself.

It is not uncommon for files to fail at this step of the process, so don't freak out! Just circle back to the narrator and get a new set. Just make sure your contract with the narrator includes any fixing of the technical files.

Any late changes will impact the timeline for publication, so make sure to allow enough time for issue resolution.

Questions:

- What kind of voice do you have in mind for your book?

- How will you find the right narrator?

- How long is your book? How many finished hours of audio will that result in? How much might the narration cost? What rate can you afford for your book?

- What kind of contract will you arrange with your narrator?

- How will you work successfully with your narrator to ensure happiness and success on both sides?

- How will you deal with the QA process?

1.6 Reasons to narrate your own audiobook

> "Words mean more than what is set
> down on paper. It takes the human voice to
> infuse them with deeper meaning."
>
> *Maya Angelou*

Most authors license their audio rights and/or work with professional narrators to produce their audiobooks, so why might you consider narrating your own work?

(1) You love audio

I presume you're reading (or listening to) this because you love audio. It's interesting to many as a growth segment in terms of author income, but if you don't love a medium, you will never master it.

When people ask me about writing a book but say they don't read, I tune them out, because they will never be successful as an author for the long term. Why would they be? They don't spend time devouring books.

The same applies to audio. Don't even think about narrating unless you enjoy the medium.

(2) Build a connection with listeners and stand out in a crowded market

There are a lot of books in the world, and more published every day, not to mention other written work in journalism and social media, plus all the different ways that people spend their time.

Voice builds connection, and in an increasingly crowded market, we all need a relationship with readers to sustain a creative career. As an example, when I released *Productivity for Authors* with a self-narrated audiobook, @Kristinglas posted the following comment on Twitter: "I'm finding @ thecreativepenn new book so helpful. I have the audiobook and it's like Joanna is giving me a personal pep talk."

With audiobooks, a listener needs to connect with the voice of the author, but also the voice of the narrator who brings the book alive. When you narrate your own work, you double down on that connection.

An author who narrates is also memorable. I became a fan of thriller author, Scott Sigler, over a decade ago when I listened to him narrate *Infected* and the subsequent books in his sci-fi/horror series. I've bought a number of his books since then and still have his voice in my head on some of the climactic scenes. I have spread the word about his books for years because he stood out by reading his stories.

(3) Improve your writing skill and characterization

Reading your work aloud can improve your writing craft.

With non-fiction, you're forced to read aloud sentences that might be full of jargon, or difficult to read or make sense of. You will **edit for content, structure, and flow**, resulting in a stronger book.

With fiction, you have to think hard about your characters, taking them off the written page and into spoken dialogue. I've ended up rewriting conversation as I read it aloud because I realized my characters wouldn't speak like that.

You will **become a better storyteller** if you perform your work because you think about the listener far more when you speak than when you write.

Regardless of genre, narration is another **line edit,** and you will pick up things even a proofreader missed when reading aloud.

(4) Create another intellectual property asset (and another stream of income) that you control

Your book is not one book. Your manuscript is an intellectual property asset that you can turn into many products and multiple streams of income.

Independent authors have mastered ebooks and print-on-demand over the last decade. We can now publish on almost every global platform and produce editions as diverse as mass-market paperback, hardback, and large print as well as ebooks and audio.

As independent authors, we control our assets, publishing them to new platforms as they become available, expanding our streams of income into the global market. Audiobooks offer another way to reach readers in a different medium and create other income streams. But the cost can be prohibitive, and royalty share deals split the revenue for years to come.

If you self-narrate your book, you can reduce costs, increase revenue, and stay in control of timing as well as take advantage of future opportunities for your work. Hiring a narrator can be expensive — usually US$200-$500 per finished hour of audio, but if you learn to do it yourself, you can produce books faster and more cheaply. Of course, you have to learn new skills and purchase equipment, but if you have a large backlist or intend to write more in the future, it may well be worth doing.

I also enjoy extending my body of work into the audio sphere. Change happens fast, and if you rely on one company, one product, or one form of income, you may find yourself struggling in a market shift. I intend to write and create for at least the next 50 years, and developing audio as part of my body of work is an exciting possibility.

(5) Increase self-confidence in performing your creative work

At the time of writing, I have still never read my fiction in public. I've spoken professionally all over the world, but I have never read so much as a line of my novels in a public venue.

I've been afraid of it for so long because it means so much. My fiction is my heart and by putting it out there, I make myself vulnerable. So I have turned down many opportunities to read or speak as my fiction persona, J.F.Penn. But slowly, as I narrate my stories for audio, I'm growing in confidence.

Audiobook narration is a performance, even if you're alone in a sound booth. You think about the listener on the other side of the microphone and you start to learn the shape of your own words. Perhaps you will see me read my fiction in public sometime in the future!

(6) Self-development

As a learning junkie, it's so much fun to discover a new skill. I narrated my first non-fiction audiobook in 2015, but since then, I've learned a lot more about the art of narration. Through voice coaching, reading and, most importantly, practice, I've discovered a whole new world of sound. I've learned more about my body and voice as an instrument, and about how to care for something I have always taken for granted.

(7) Increase exposure and marketing within a genre

I only narrate my own books right now, but I am considering narration of other books related to my brand. Audio listeners become a fan of the narrator, not just the author, and will often follow them from book to book, so narration in a niche can be a way to market your other work.

It's certainly a way off yet, as it takes time and energy to narrate and edit, as well as a budget for mastering, but it's on my longer-term plan. This may become easier with voice licensing as covered in chapter 3.6 on Artificial intelligence and the future of voice.

Questions:

- Why might you consider narrating your own audiobook/s?

- How do you feel about someone whose voice you like? What attributes do you ascribe to them? Do you connect more to that person because of their voice?

- Do you have the time, budget, and attitude to invest in learning about self-narration?

- What might be your first project?

1.7 Audiobook narration tips

> "Learn more about this wonderful instrument
> you were born to use, put your fears behind you
> and go and make some noise."
>
> *Cerys Matthews, This is a Voice*

Have you been to a book launch or literary festival and sat through a deathly monotone author reading? Or watched with empathy as a writer stumbles over their own words, sweating and pale-faced behind the mic as they stare at the page instead of connecting with the audience?

Writing for the page is a completely different skill to performing for an audience — and it is performing, not reading, which is the mistake most authors make. If you want to learn audiobook narration, you have to be willing to perform your book. That doesn't mean you need to be fake or ham it up in any way, but you have to think about the listener, about the person on the other side of the microphone. It's not about what's going on in your head, it's about what's going on in theirs. This mindset shift can be a challenge at first, but with time and practice, you will get there!

In this chapter, I'll go through my tips from personal experience after narrating five non-fiction audiobooks and several fiction short stories. For much more detail from a highly-experienced narrator, I recommend *Storyteller: How to be an Audiobook Narrator* by Lorelei King and Ali

Muirden. The audiobook version is fantastic, as Lorelei gives examples of the kinds of voice issues you might experience as a narrator, and it's also available in print.

Do you really want to narrate?

The last chapter presented compelling reasons for self-narration, so maybe you are raring to go, but it's worth stopping a moment to reconsider before you buy equipment or hire a studio.

Like writing a book or independently publishing, you will learn much more by trying it yourself, so start by reading text aloud. Pick a book from your shelf or select some of your own written work, then read it aloud as if you had a microphone in front of you.

Forgive your initial stumbling and mistakes — there will be a lot! Don't worry. This is not serious. No one else is here. There is no recording, so just give it a go.

Once you've read a few paragraphs, stop and consider how it went.

How did it feel? Are you excited to learn more? Are you willing to practice and learn the skills necessary to create your own audiobook? If yes, read on.

Voice confidence

Feeling self-doubt around your ability to narrate is completely normal, and most authors have little experience, so you are not alone if you have some concerns at this stage.

I'm an introvert, and I like a quiet world around me. I will often listen to rain and thunderstorms through my noise-canceling headphones to mute the surrounding sound. I get stressed in airports when the cacophony of noise overwhelms me. I wear earplugs to sleep every night even though I live in a quiet area. My life is usually hushed, so I had to really switch gears in order to use my voice effectively.

I've been podcasting for a decade now and a paid professional speaker for just as long, so I am used to the sound of my voice and performing in public, but I still took voice coaching lessons for audiobook narration. Reading my own work felt like an entirely different prospect, and I particularly wanted coaching around my fiction in order to differentiate characters.

Even if you have no fear and doubt around your voice, coaching can help you improve. You will expand your range and play with your voice instrument. You will learn techniques for warming up, stretches to expand your chest and lungs, and ways to limber up your throat and tongue. Check out workshops for actors, as they often have audiobook narration classes, or hire a voice coach for one-on-one consulting in person or over Skype.

I also recommend *This is a Voice: 99 Exercises to Train, Project and Harness the Power of your Voice* by Jeremy Fisher and Gillyanne Kayes, which will help you recognize how powerful your voice really is.

Make sure your environment is ready for narration

Before you start narrating, consider this checklist:

Are you recording in a quiet environment? Stand still and listen. What noises can you hear? Does the microphone pick them up?

Have you made sure you won't be interrupted?

Have you turned off the Wi-Fi on your phone or tablet or watch? This is not just about interruption by human sound. It's also about the noise of a signal that you can't necessarily hear.

Have you checked the levels on your microphone? Do a sound test and check the settings. I have two settings marked on my microphone for gain levels: One for podcasting where I am more animated and speak extemporaneously, and one for audiobooks, which are more of a straight performance.

Have you recorded 10-15 seconds of room tone with no other noises? This is required for the technical files but also enables cleaner edits and mastering that can be used to cover any sound. I usually do this at the beginning and end of every chapter recording and hold my breath while staying very still and counting silently.

What do you read from?

Some narrators prefer to prepare books on paper, for example, highlighting characters, adding commas for breath, writing down pronunciations in the margin. They will then perform the book with the paper copy but will minimize shuffling and other noises as they turn the page as that will need editing later.

Other narrators use a tablet or e-reading device, for example, an iPad or a Kindle. I use an iPad with the iAnnotate app for PDF files, which enables me to highlight in different colors and write notes for narration. I can also add notes in the middle of the read if I need to go back and update the master manuscript later.

What if you make a mistake while narrating?

You *will* make mistakes while narrating. That is 100% going to happen, and it's not a big deal. When you notice it, stop and start the sentence again. You (or your audiobook editor) can edit out the mistakes later.

Say the line.

You mess it up.

Say it again.

And again. Make sure you use the same energy so it can be easily edited with the rest of the paragraph, or start the whole section again if you need to reset.

If you keep getting a line wrong, consider why that might be happening. Is it poorly written? If you wrote the book, can you re-edit the sentence to make it easier to read?

Is it a tongue-twister of a sentence? Or maybe you're just tired from concentrating too long. Take a break and come back to it later.

Remember to laugh at yourself and play around with saying things out loud in different ways. You can sigh and make other noises, too, especially if you're alone. Anything to warm up your voice so you can get that sentence out!

Professional audiobook narrators working in a studio sometimes have a director who will pick up problems, mispronunciations, and extraneous sounds like mouth noise.

Narrators working from a home studio or authors self-narrating will not use a director, so any issues have to be picked up in the quality control process and fixed later.

Remember, audiobook narration is not live, so you can repeat the process until you are happy with it. This is another reason I like having a home studio, as there is no one to witness the number of times I have to read certain sentences. Sometimes I make so many mistakes I just delete the file and do it again another day. A clean straight read makes editing far less painful!

Your ability to read straight passages without mistakes will impact the time it takes to record the raw audio. Professional audiobook narrators can go for a long period without edits and breaks, whereas new narrators or those of us doing it for our own books will take a lot longer.

Let's get physical!

Audiobook narration is surprisingly tiring. When I recorded my first audiobook back in 2015, I thought there was something wrong with me. I would leave the studio drained and exhausted after each session and swore never to do it again. Eventually, I discovered that everyone feels this way, and it takes time to build up stamina for narration.

After all, it's physically hard work to stand and concentrate on written text for hours. You can sit in some studios, but I prefer to stand as it keeps my energy focused. Even if you sit, you'll have to make sure your posture remains consistent as it impacts your voice quality.

It's also hard work to speak and use your voice for hours at a time, especially if you're an introvert and work from home when you might not talk so much.

This is important to keep in mind so you can **manage your energy levels,** which affect your voice and your performance. You have to maintain the same energy throughout the book, which might mean scheduling four sessions of two hours each in a studio on different days instead of eight hours in one day.

If you have your own recording setup, you can **work when it's best for you and take breaks.** I narrate in the morning and usually do a couple of chapters, then take a break, then do one more session before I'm done. I'm never in my booth for more than a couple of hours in total, with several breaks for water and to rest my eyes and stretch.

Body and mouth noises

When you narrate, you need to become more attuned to the noises of your body. Tummy rumbles, lip-smacking, throat clearing, clothes rustling, jewelry jangling. All picked up by the microphone and probably needing a retake. Here are some tips for making sure the only sound is your voice.

Eat something light before narration but leave enough time, so any digestive noises calm down. Don't skip eating or your tummy will rumble. I once tried narration while intermittent fasting, but my digestive system was just too noisy.

Avoid 'claggy' foods like too much dairy, peanut butter, or other things that stick in the mouth and can make wet sounds. Many narrators recommend bananas for energy and green apples for getting rid of mouth noise.

Stay hydrated. Mouth sounds can be worse when you're dehydrated. Coffee beforehand is not recommended, but I am a coffeeholic, so I drink it black and also have room temperature water nearby to sip and swill. Avoid fizzy drinks as they can lead to burping. I also use lip balm but wipe away excess moisture to avoid lip sounds.

If you have an **itchy throat** or a cough, record another day if possible. If you really have to record, drink Throat Coat tea, or anything with licorice. You can also put a throat sweet into water so it dissolves and sip that.

Always start a sentence with your mouth open, or you will get a lip smack at the beginning.

Use a **pop filter** in front of your microphone. It will stop 'plosives' like 'p' or 'b' which send air over the microphone.

If you are still getting a lot of noise, **stand further back from the mic** and play with the gain. Experiment with different levels and see what works best for you.

There may be other noises in your environment. Make sure you wear soft fabrics, as some clothes make a noise if you move. Take off any jangling jewelry. If you stand to narrate, don't bounce or rub on the carpet or make excessive movements where you might bang the mic. If you read from paper, prepare it so you can see several pages in advance and hand-write any extra words on the bottom of one page, so you don't have to turn the page mid-sentence.

The best tip is to **just give it a go and listen to the noises you make while narrating**. You'll discover your quirks quickly and learn how to avoid them. If there is noise, no worries, just say the line again.

Look at the mic as if it were a person

Before you start reading, look at the mic. **Imagine it is a person listening**. Smile at it and direct energy from behind your eyes.

A **smile** can be heard in a voice as can other emotions.

As you read, look up now and then to refocus on the mic, which represents the listener. **Remember that it is all about them.**

This might sound crazy, but it really works and you can hear the difference.

You don't have to do voices or accents when you self-narrate

This was one of my great stumbling blocks. I thought that in order to narrate fiction, I'd have to learn how to do accents and different voices. But you can do a straight read, positioning yourself more in the storyteller tradition.

Of course, there are brilliant audiobooks by talented actors doing different voices. But there are also great audiobooks narrated with one voice with no attempt to differentiate.

It's all in the attitude, the emotional truth and energy behind your narration. You need to act in the sense of portraying the story, but you don't need to do fake voices.

The narrator should disappear behind the story, and a bad accent can drop people out of the fictive dream. So if you're not great at voices, just stick with a straight read.

Questions:

- How confident are you at reading or performing your written work? What can you do to increase your confidence?

- What will you do if you make a mistake during narration?

- How can you make sure that you maintain energy and a personal connection to the listener while recording?

- How will you prepare yourself and your environment?

- What can you do to reduce extraneous noise?

- Record yourself narrating a piece of your work. Listen back for any noises in the recording. What do you notice?

- If you're hiring a professional studio, what can you do to make sure you get the most out of your time?

1.8 Recording studio options

Your finished audiobook must conform to specific technical standards and must also provide a good listening experience. Much of this is controlled by the editing and mastering of the files, but if you don't have good-quality raw audio, then editing will be expensive or even impossible.

If you hire a narrator, this is not your problem, because they guarantee finished files that conform to the required standard, but if you narrate yourself, then you need to record in a decent sound environment.

It's important to record the whole audiobook in the same place, so however you start, make sure to finish the book in the same way. This ensures that your baseline audio — the room sound — is the same and makes it easier to edit and master later. There are several options.

(1) Hire a local studio

You will find audio studios in most towns and cities, primarily used by radio stations, independent musicians, and other voice talent.

You can usually hire an audio producer as well as the venue, who can help with the editing and mastering of the files, although, of course, this will cost more than just hiring the site.

Studio hire can be the best idea when you're starting out with narration because if you decide you hate it and never want to record again, then you won't have over-invested in equipment.

Since audiobook narration takes stamina, I recommend booking several sessions of a few hours each over multiple days instead of trying to get everything done in one or two straight days. This ensures that you keep your energy levels consistent across the recording.

(2) Bootstrap a recording environment

No one will see you record your audiobook, so as long as it sounds good, you can do whatever you like.

I know one narrator who recorded under a thick blanket at his kitchen table, emerging for fresh air now and then. Author and narrator M.L. Buchman describes some basic setups in his book, *Narrate and Record Your Own Audiobook*, which includes a blanket over a clothes rack and a small shower stall covered with audio blankets.

Find a space with as much padding as possible — no wooden floors or high ceilings or busy roads — then use blankets and soft furnishings to prevent any extra noise. This is a good option if you are in rental accommodation or somewhere too small for a permanent booth. You'll have to set it up every time, but each audiobook won't take too long to narrate, and you can dismantle it afterward. Take pictures of the setup and technical settings so you can reproduce it quickly next time.

(3) Buy a pre-made studio setup

There are lots of options for buying a studio setup, ranging from the cheaper mobile recording studio — basically a padded box — through to a full-construction stand-alone room with fans, lighting, and sound-proofing.

These options can range from several hundred dollars to many thousands, so consider what your needs are and how you plan to make back your investment.

My home studio

In my previous rental flat, I recorded in a walk-in ward-robe. I stuck some foam soundboards to the walls, and my clothes deadened any extraneous sound. This gave me passable audio for my first few audiobooks, but I had to set it up every time, and the sound wasn't perfect.

When we bought a house, I decided to invest in an audio booth. The professional setup was too expensive and also would be hard to deconstruct if we wanted to move. So I hired a carpenter to make a wooden frame and covered it with acoustic sound blankets. It cost about one-tenth of the pro setup, and the sound is fantastic.

I use a BlueYeti microphone on a stand with a pop filter and shock mount. I have a basic music stand to rest my iPad on and a bar stool for my laptop as well as a small light. If it gets too hot in the summer, I pull open the blankets and put a fan inside between recording sessions.

You can find my full setup with links to the equipment at:

TheCreativePenn.com/homestudio

Your choice of microphone and studio setup will differ from mine and there is an incredible range of options. You get to decide your budget and also how geeky you want to get around audio.

Questions:

- What will you use for your recording studio? Why are you making this choice?

1.9 Audiobook recording, editing and production

This is not a technical book, and I am not a professional sound engineer. Although I love audio, I'm interested in the creative side and the resulting income, and I outsource anything technical. In this chapter, I explain your options for creating your audiobook.

What are the audiobook submission requirements?

At the time of writing, the ACX audio submission requirements are as follows:

Your submitted audiobook must:

- Be consistent in overall sound and formatting

- Be comprised of all mono or all stereo files

- Include opening and closing credits

- Include a retail sample that is between one and five minutes long

- Be recorded by a human

Each uploaded audio file must also contain only one chapter, have room tone at the beginning and the end, be free of extraneous sound, and adhere to exact sound specifications.

ACX, Findaway Voices, and other services use similar requirements, so if you stick to these, you should be fine.

If you don't understand some of the technicalities, don't worry. You can work with a professional sound engineer to master your files, as I do.

Recording your audiobook

You will edit your audiobook later, but the quality of your recording is critical, as this will determine how much post-processing you will have to do and how expensive this might be.

I use a Blue Yeti microphone and Amadeus Pro software with a MacBook Pro inside my home booth for recording.

Many authors use Audacity software as it is free and for the PC as well as the Mac. Pro Tools and Adobe Audition are also recommended.

File management

File management is a critical part of the process, as you don't want to lose any work, and you don't want to have to re-record whole chunks of audio, especially if you hired a studio.

As you record each chapter, save your original raw files with all the mistakes, out-takes, bodily noises, and interruptions into a Raw Audio folder.

Back up those files. I save everything to Dropbox, and I also have the raw files on an external hard drive.

Copy the raw files to a new folder for editing, so you always have the originals, then edit the copies. Some of the out-takes might be useful for edits, but are also needed in case you mess up the editing process and have to start again.

Once the files are edited, move them into another folder: Ready for Production.

My sound engineer copies all those files into another drive, so we have yet another copy. Then he masters them to produce the final files for upload and distribution.

Editing your audiobook

The recording software can also be used for editing the files, and most people will use one of the programs mentioned above.

I open my manuscript and follow through with my own narration in Amadeus Pro, deleting any repeated sections, noises, coughing, mistakes and anything else, so that I finish each chapter with a smooth read. I might find some issues that need re-recording, but usually I have acknowledged my mistakes in the recording process and fixed them at the time.

My edits are usually just highlighting a section of the audio and clicking Delete. I don't do any splicing of files, inserts, or anything more technical at this stage, so it's a pretty basic process.

You can outsource this editing, but it is quite time-intensive, so it can cost quite a bit, plus, you will miss out on a chance to learn. Listening to yourself can be painful, but it's the best way to see what you need to do to improve for next time.

Mastering and production

The files need final editing and mastering to bring them up to the required standard for distribution as per the guidelines for each service.

If you want to do this yourself, I recommend *Narrate and Record Your Own Audiobook* by M.L. Buchman, as it goes into detail on the technical side of preparing your files for submission to the audio platforms.

I prefer to outsource this step and work with a sound engineer to master my files, so all I have to do is upload them later.

If you record your audiobook in a local studio, it's likely that you will be able to find sound engineers who can work with the ACX guidelines, even if they usually work with radio or musicians. You can also look for freelancers on sites like Upwork.com or PeoplePerHour.com, as well as have a look at the professional audiobook associations like the Audio Publishers Association.

Questions:

- What software will you use for recording and editing your files?

- How will you manage your files so you don't lose any work?

- Are you interested in learning the technical side of sound engineering, or do you want to outsource the mastering and production of your files?

1.10 How to self-publish an audiobook

Once you have your finished files ready for distribution, there are a number of companies you can use to independently publish your audiobook. Your choices will depend on where you are in the world, as not all services are available globally.

I use ACX alongside Findaway Voices for my audiobooks, so those are the companies I'll focus on here.

ACX

ACX.com is a marketplace where rights-holders (authors, publishers, agents, etc.) can connect with narrators and producers to enable audiobook production. It's an Amazon company, and audiobooks produced through the site are sold on Amazon, Audible and iTunes.

You have to legally own the rights to use ACX; for example, you're an independent author who self-publishes, or a traditionally published author who has not licensed audio rights.

At the time of writing, ACX.com is only available to authors in the US, UK, Canada and Ireland, but hopefully, it will expand to other territories over time as audiobooks continue to grow. You can also use Findaway Voices as covered below this section if you are outside of these countries.

Log into ACX with your normal Amazon login and claim your book

Search with the Amazon ASIN, the number that Amazon assigns to every book on the store, or the book title and then claim your book, so it is assigned to your ACX account. This will be available as an option as soon as your book is on pre-order. If you want to launch your audiobook at the same time as your ebook and print book, use a pre-order period that allows for the amount of time it takes to produce and publish an audiobook as covered in chapter 1.11.

Enter the book details for the narrator

ACX will pull information from your ebook profile, but you will need to add notes on sales and your author platform, which is particularly important if you want to attract an experienced narrator, or if you want to do royalty share deals.

You also need to include a sample for the audition and specify what type of voice you want. For example, an African-American adult male vs. a young adult female would suit two different narrators.

You only need to load your audiobook cover by the time you publish, but adding it early might attract more narrators to audition for the project. I have mine designed at the same time as the ebook and print book covers. They have the same design element and font, but audiobook covers are square, even in digital format, presumably because of CD covers in the past.

Decide on the contract and exclusivity

At this stage, you must choose the type of deal you'd like to do with a narrator — pay outright or a royalty-split deal. The latter is a seven-year contract and you will need to be exclusive with ACX.

If you self-narrate or you have hired a narrator at the finished hour rate, there is only one choice at the contract stage — whether you go exclusive or non-exclusive with ACX for distribution.

If you go exclusive, you receive a higher royalty rate, but your audiobook will only be available on Amazon, Audible, and iTunes. This is also a seven-year contract, but if you own the rights, you can email ACX after one year and ask to move to a non-exclusive contract.

If you go non-exclusive, you receive a lower royalty rate, but you can also publish your audiobook on other platforms and sell direct from your website. You have complete control.

If you are exclusive with ACX, your audiobook will only be available to those who listen on Audible and iTunes. You're missing out on other global markets and companies which are expanding at an incredible rate like Storytel, Scribd, Kobo Audio and more, with new services emerging all the time.

You also miss out on library distribution if you're exclusive on ACX, and you can't sell direct or use a promotional service like Chirp from BookBub. These may be small income streams at first, but over time, as you develop an audiobook ecosystem and the market keeps expanding, these could overtake your ACX royalties.

Findaway Voices

FindawayVoices.com can help match you with a narrator, or you can publish your own files separately. They have a royalty share option as well as a pay per finished hour contract. You can set the price for your audiobook separately for the retail and library markets, and you can use their Authors Direct app to sell audio direct to listeners.

Their tagline is 'Take back your freedom,' because the creator has the opportunity to reach listeners on global audiobook platforms and set their own price.

Most of the features are available to authors globally, but some are being rolled out to different markets over time.

Kobo Writing Life (KWL) Audio

You can publish audiobooks directly through Kobo Writing Life, and this will make your audiobook eligible for different kinds of promotion. Kobo.com sells audiobooks to its readers, but Kobo also works with Overdrive for library distribution, as well as having distribution deals with Walmart and other companies. You can reach the same markets through Findaway, but the additional promotion may make it worthwhile to go direct to KWL.

Your audiobook. Your choice.

I prefer to go wide with audio as much as possible, so I choose non-exclusive for my English-language audiobooks. However, when I was starting out as an author, with less money to invest, I did exclusive, royalty-split deals, so it's completely your choice.

I use ACX with a non-exclusive contract for Amazon and Audible distribution and then use Findaway Voices to reach wider markets. I'm pulling all my books out of ACX exclusivity when the royalty-split contracts come up for renewal.

There are other companies that can help you get your books into audio and, of course, you may choose to license your rights to an audiobook production company. Whatever you choose, make sure you understand where the audiobook will be distributed and how your royalties will work for the long term.

Pricing

When you publish through ACX, they set the price. It is calculated based on audiobook length and can also change based on the various pricing mechanisms and promotions used by Audible.

For example, a subscriber gets one credit a month for $9.99 and can 'buy' a $40 audiobook with that credit. There are also various other discounting options for audiobook listeners that mean they don't pay full retail price for an audiobook. The royalty statement from ACX includes a breakdown of all these different variations.

When you publish through Findaway Voices, you can set your own price for both retail and library sales. You also have an opportunity to do promotional pricing, which helps with marketing.

So, if you want to control your own price, go with Findaway.

Physical sales of audiobooks

In 2018, the Audio Publishers Association survey announced that 91% of audiobook sales in the USA were digital. While the rest of the world lags behind by a few years, the global use of mobile devices means that these numbers will continue to grow. So while you can manufacture and sell your audiobooks on CD with companies like CDBaby, you have to consider whether it is worth it. Personally, I choose to distribute my audiobooks in digital format only.

Questions:

- What are the different options for self-publishing an audiobook? What are the pros and cons for each?

- What would suit your project right now, and how might that change in the future?

1.11 How long does an audiobook take to produce?

Independent authors are used to publishing at speed. Once you have an edited manuscript, you can upload your ebook and have it for sale the same day, and print books can be available almost as fast. But the audiobook process can only start once you have a finished manuscript, and the timelines will depend on several factors.

Narrator availability

Great narrators, like great editors, are often booked up well in advance and will have to schedule your book into their timelines. If you have someone in mind and you can control your creative process, then book them in advance but make sure to meet your deadline.

Even if you're narrating yourself, you still have to schedule the time.

Narrator experience, pick-ups, and QA process

An experienced narrator can record a standard audiobook pretty fast, especially if they work with someone else to do the edits, mastering, and production of the files.

But you also need to make sure your time is available to do the QA process. The project cannot be completed until you sign it off, and the narrator might have to do some pickups or re-recording for any issues.

The QA process will take at least as long as the finished book but usually allow more time to stop, note down any issues, and continue. For example, an eight-hour book might take nine hours to QA, and you are unlikely to do that in one session.

The files will need mastering according to the technical specifications, and this also adds time to the process.

Upload and technical checks

Once the finished files are available, upload them to the distribution platforms and add metadata, cover, and pricing where necessary. This only takes an hour or so, but you need to make sure you are happy with everything before finally approving and submitting the files. I usually listen to the beginning of every chapter to make sure they are all labeled correctly and in the right order.

Once you submit the audiobook, it can take a few weeks to appear in the stores, and that timing can't be controlled or hurried along. If there are technical errors, you'll hear back within a couple of days. If the project is accepted, you'll get an email when it is available in the stores.

Can you launch an audiobook at the same time as other formats?

Many authors publish audiobooks after the ebook and print editions, but in terms of marketing, it's ideal to have your audiobook available at launch, so readers have a choice of formats from day one.

Allow a month of pre-order from the upload of finished files to ACX and Findaway to be sure of making it on time.

I now delay my ebook and print publication until later so I can market at the same time. However, I have only managed this organized simultaneous release a couple of times over 30+ books, so you can be successful either way!

Questions:

- How long will it take for the production of your audiobook?

- What are some of the aspects that might delay your audiobook?

- How will you time the releases of your other editions so you can market the audiobook simultaneously?

1.12 How do audiobook readers discover audiobooks?

I'm a writer, but I'm a reader first. I buy and read three to five books per week, and have many more on my bookshelves that I have yet to touch. If you're a bibliophile like me, your To Read pile will be just as large!

But my reading habits have changed significantly over the last few years. From 2010 - 2017, I read 99% of the time on my Kindle and occasionally bought print books. Since 2017, I've been reading far more non-fiction in audio format and also buying hardback editions of books I find useful and want to keep for reference. I still read fiction in ebook format only. My husband is the opposite. He binges on long fiction audiobook series, preferably over 30 hours per book.

This chapter is a snapshot of how our household finds audiobooks to feed our addiction. It is just anecdotal but might prove useful in understanding audio-first consumers before we get into the details of marketing.

Note: We are in the UK and use Audible as the primary app, but behavior across other audiobook retailers might be similar.

Browsing online bookstores

I shop for books almost every day. One of my favorite pastimes is browsing the Kindle store, looking for new books released in the last 30 days in the genres I enjoy. If I find a non-fiction book that I want, I check to see if there's an audiobook edition. If there is, I'll click over, listen to the sample and add it to my Wishlist for when my credit comes through.

There is a recommendation engine within Audible, although it is not as comprehensive as the Kindle store, so I will often browse on Amazon, find a book I want and then click through to audio from there. I rarely browse Audible itself, although that may change over time as their recommendations improve.

Browsing physical bookstores

I go into bookstores at least once a week and usually walk out with a book or two (or six!), as well as notes of others I want to buy. If I find a book that would be better in audio, I make a note and look it up later, then add it to my Wishlist.

BookBub and email blasts about cheap ebooks

This is only relevant for Amazon and Audible if the book is available with Whispersync. If you own the ebook, you can get the accompanying audio for a lot cheaper than a credit or buying outright. So if you download a cheap ebook on a BookBub deal, you can immediately upgrade to the audio. You can also find matching audiobooks with Amazon

Matchmaker. My husband particularly enjoys doing this for long fantasy series.

Email blasts about audiobooks

BookBub also has Chirp for discounted audiobook deals, but it is only available in some countries. There are also online magazines like Audiofile, which email about audiobooks every week.

Recommendations, deals and sales

Audible emails me at least once a week with deals and sales on audiobooks I have on my Wishlist, or notifies me of things I might like. For example, I heard about Bill Bryson's book, *The Body: A Guide for Occupants* through Audible and added it to my Wishlist, then bought it when my credit came through.

I will sometimes buy a pack of three credits for a reduced rate if there are multiple audiobooks I want — as with books in any format, this means I have a number in my queue that I haven't read yet!

Podcasts

I get a lot of non-fiction book recommendations from podcasts. I listen to around ten shows per week in different niches, and if I like an interview with a guest, I will buy their book to learn more. But if it's not available in audio, I may not buy it at all. This change in my reading behavior is driving me to ensure I have all editions available on launch for my own non-fiction books, in particular.

Media recommendations

I monitor lists of awards in the non-fiction space, especially, for example, science prizes or lists of recommended books in reputable newspapers. I read a lot of business books in audio.

Personal recommendations

If I love an audiobook, I will rave about it far more than a print book or ebook. I've told countless people how much I love *Underland* by Rob Macfarlane. It is an incredibly beautiful audiobook. If someone else recommends an audiobook, I often sample it because that experience is so rare. An excellent audiobook can really spread by word of mouth.

Alexa BookFinder

I had laser eye surgery in mid-2019 and had to keep my eyes closed in the recovery period, so I binge-listened to audiobooks for days on end. I kept my Echo Dot by the bed so I could ask Alexa to play various audiobooks, or the radio, or play a word game.

You can ask Alexa to recommend books to you on the smart speaker or through your device. Use the wake phrase, "Alexa, open Book Finder," for a selection of trending listens, bestsellers, and personal recommendations.

Questions:

- If you listen to audiobooks right now, how do you discover what to listen to next? Ask your friends and family for a wider response.

1.13 How to market audiobooks

The audiobook is just another format, so while there are things you can do to market them specifically, any general marketing activities will also promote your audiobook. For example, if you speak at a literary festival or conference and mention your book, some in the audience may prefer to buy it in audio. Here are some things you can do to market audiobooks, in particular.

(1) Link to and promote all editions

When your audiobook becomes available, make sure you link it to the other editions on Amazon. You can request the link through Amazon Author Central if it hasn't appeared automatically within a few days of publication.

Create a link on Books2Read.com for all the places people can buy your books, including the various audiobook stores. For example, Books2Read.com/makealiving will take you to links for the ebook and audiobook editions for *How to Make a Living with your Writing*.

(2) Create a landing page on your website for audio and link to the various sites

Make it easy for audio listeners to find you. I have landing pages per book, which include the links to the audiobook retailers. I also have a page for audio specifically, with samples.

This page should be easy to say out loud when you do podcast or radio interviews, for example, TheCreative-Penn.com/audio

You can create and use Bounty links for your books. These are unique URLs for your book and can provide extra income if readers use them for the first book they buy on Audible. They are unlimited, and I use them by default on my website.

If you use a sidebar on your main site, or widgets at the bottom, make sure your audio links are prominent to anyone who lands on your page.

(3) Make sure you have an Audible Author Page

If you have books on Audible, you can also have an Audible Author page that lists all your books and includes some information from your Amazon Author Central page. You can then promote this to Audible listeners specifically so they can find all your books.

(4) Use audiograms

An audiogram is an audio snippet played as a small video with a moving waveform over an image. Excerpt snippets from your audiobook and use a tool like Headliner app to create a shareable video that you can use on social media, embed on your website, or use on video platforms.

You can play an audiogram from *Productivity for Authors* on Twitter at:

TheCreativePenn.com/audiogram

(5) Use social media to share images and quotes

You can use Canva.com to create appropriately sized images for the various social media platforms. This could be quotes from your audiobook, a picture of a mobile phone with headphones and your book cover, or another image that links through to your audiobook. Share on Twitter and Facebook, pin on Pinterest, and use everywhere you interact online. Remember to link to your audiobook or your main audio page.

You can also use SoundCloud.com to create shareable audio samples that link back to your buy page. You can embed these onto your website or use on social media.

For example, check out my thriller, *Valley of Dry Bones,* at:

Soundcloud.com/jfpenn/valley-of-dry-bones

(6) Use paid advertising

If you link your audiobook edition with your ebook and print editions, you can use Amazon Advertising on certain stores to send traffic to your book. If you publish through KDP, click on Promote and Advertise and choose the store on which you want to advertise.

You can also use Facebook Advertising to target audiobook listeners or fans of Audible, iTunes, or other platforms and use country-specific links.

There are lots of other paid advertising opportunities available. Just make sure you learn the best way to use any platform and keep an eye on cost as well as revenue.

(7) Include audio in your email autoresponder sequence

All authors should build an email list. It's an essential part of book marketing and a way to future-proof your career by always having an independent method to reach readers.

If you don't have a website or email list yet, check out my tutorials at:

TheCreativePenn.com/authorwebsite

If you have an email list already, you can share news of your audiobook release and send snippets so people can listen. You can also create an autoresponder sequence of emails sent after readers sign up, offering them promotional audio codes and linking through to your audiobook sales page.

Some email services provide a way to tag customers when they click on links, so you can find out which formats people buy and target them more specifically down the track.

You can also share MP3 audio files with links through BookFunnel.com, which many indie authors already use to distribute ebooks. You could use a sample of a full audio-book, a short story, or anything to get listeners interested.

(8) Use giveaway codes to get reviews

ACX provides Promo Codes for books published with an exclusive deal. You can generate the codes from your ACX sales dashboard and send them to your email subscribers or use them in giveaways to get reviews. Each code can be redeemed for one audiobook.

You can also get giveaway codes on Findaway Voices for Authors Direct, which is also only available to selected markets.

(9) Market to libraries or library listeners

If you use Findaway Voices, you can make your audiobook available in libraries, and this is a win/win situation for you and your readers. It's free for them to listen, and you still get paid. It's also good for libraries to license independent books because they are often cheaper to buy and/or use a pay-per-checkout model. You get a smaller payment per checkout, but the library is more likely to digitally stock the book, giving readers more options.

Tell your audience that they can get your book for free at the library. They just need to ask the librarian to order it from the catalog. *[Yes, you can get my books for free at the library. Just ask!]*

(10) Promote your ebook in order to sell more audio

Once you own the ebook on Amazon, you can upgrade to the audiobook for a lower price, so BookBub deals can be used by audiobook listeners to get great value deals, as my husband does with his favorite fantasy series.

Other ebook promotion services are useful as it is sometimes challenging to get BookBub deals.

You can also encourage listeners to use Amazon Audible Matchmaker, which scans your Kindle books and finds matching audiobooks.

Tell your audience about these options so they can get your audiobooks on special. After all, every sale is a good sale!

(11) Use audiobook promotion services

Discounted ebook services are a well-established way to promote free or cheap ebooks, but there are fewer options for audiobooks, although this will likely change as the market continues to grow.

BookBub's Chirp could be the game-changer for audiobook promotion, but at the time of writing, it is still in the early days and not open to authors in every country. It is for non-exclusive audiobooks, and they partner with Findaway Voices, where you can apply for promotions through the Marketing tab. Check it out at Chirpbooks.com

AudiobookBoom.com enables you to reach a list of audiobook listeners. You provide review codes, and some listeners may leave a review, which can help sales.

Audiofile Magazine has options for audiobook reviews and advertising at audiofilemagazine.com

The Audio Publishers Association has promotional opportunities and also lists resources, reviewers and more on their site at Audiopub.org

(12) Upload an audiobook trailer or sample chapter on YouTube

I used to think that YouTube was just for video content, but it turns out that many people use it as a channel for listening to podcasts, audiobooks, and music. Although I've been doing video on YouTube.com/thecreativepenn since 2008, I moved to audio-only podcasting in early 2019, and my subscribers have continued growing.

Upload a sample chapter with the visual background of your audiobook cover. Include links in the description to the audiobook stores. If you own the rights, you could even upload the whole book and use ad revenue to monetize it.

You can see a sample chapter of *Successful Self-Publishing* on YouTube at:

TheCreativePenn.com/samplechapter

(13) Use QR codes to link directly to your audiobook

QR codes can be used with cellphone cameras to link directly to a website page or your audiobook page on a retailer. There are plenty of free sites online you can use to generate a QR code. Then you can add them to physical marketing assets like business cards or postcards to be used at live events, as well as distributing online.

This QR code goes to my audiobook landing page in the print and ebook editions of the book. Use your phone camera to scan the image.

(14) Audio sells audio. Pitch for podcast interviews or buy advertising.

The Audio Publishers Association 2018 survey reported that 55% of audiobook listeners in the US had also listened to a podcast in the last month.

This isn't surprising, because people who like listening to audio don't just listen to audiobooks. I might swap between several different podcasts and audiobooks during the day, depending on what I'm doing and what I want to listen to in the moment. I also find a lot of audiobooks through interviews with authors on podcasts.

Part 2 covers podcasting in detail, but for now, think about the podcasts you listen to or research the best podcasts in your niche. How could you feature on those shows?

(15) Hire a narrator with a following

Some narrators are so well-known that people follow them from book to book, which bakes in marketing from day one.

They will be more expensive, but if you have a dream narrator in mind for your niche, ask them about availability and rates.

(16) Create more audio products

If you only have full-length audiobooks, **try offering shorter works** like short stories or short non-fiction. These will be cheaper to produce and purchase, and if you put the ebook out for free or 99c, people can try your audio more easily. You can also publish these shorter audio works for free on YouTube or SoundCloud.

On the other end of the scale, create **audiobook boxsets** enabling you to reach those people who want a long audiobook. Boxsets are great for promotional deals as they are easier to discount and still make money on, plus they are great value for the listener.

Questions:

- What are some of the ways you could market your audiobook? Note down any quick wins you can achieve in the next month as well as a plan for long-term marketing.

1.14 The money side of audiobooks

Audiobooks are a growth market, but they are definitely not easy money, especially as an independent author. If you do decide to go ahead and invest, then each completed audiobook is an asset that can earn money for the long term, and once you have a backlist, listeners may purchase more than one book.

In this chapter, I outline how the money works for audio, and, as ever, there are several options.

License your audiobook rights

If you're traditionally published, check your contract. You may have already licensed your audiobook rights, so it's worth following up with your publisher if it hasn't been produced. If your book is not available as an audiobook, you will never get any further royalties from it.

If you haven't licensed your audiobook rights, this is definitely an option, especially if you're an established author with a fanbase. Pitch one of the many professional audiobook producers, or you may even get an offer from them directly if your book is selling a lot.

If you license the rights, you will usually get an advance and may get royalties later, depending on the contract you negotiate and your sales success. There are no upfront costs for you.

While some authors can negotiate six figures for audiobook rights, anecdotal evidence suggests it's usually a few thousand dollars advance and a 10-30% royalty. Contracts can be term-limited, for example, rights revert after ten years.

I would absolutely sign a licensing deal with an excellent audiobook producer given the right contract. Just make sure you understand what you're signing. For more on contracts, read *Closing the Deal ... on Your Terms: Agents, Contracts and Other Considerations* by Kristine Kathryn Rusch, and *The Guide to Publishing Audiobooks: How to Produce and Sell an Audiobook* by Jessica Kaye.

The business mindset of an independent author

If you want to stay independent, you have to consider your audiobook as an intellectual property asset that you create for long-term income, as your investment will not return money instantly. You do not know how the future will turn out, so you have to plan and make the best decision for your situation.

Compare the following examples:

- Author A licenses her audiobook rights in a ten-year contract and receives US$2,000 advance, but no further royalties as the book does not earn out

- Author B pays $200 per finished hour for the production of a seven-hour audiobook, an initial upfront cost of $1,400

- Author B then receives $50 per month for the same ten-year period, giving a total of US$6,000 income, resulting in US$4,600 profit, more than double the amount of Author A

Of course, there are far too many variables to consider for every possible situation. You can only make an educated guess as to what sales might come over the long term and have a marketing plan for your audiobooks to maximize the likelihood of sales and a positive return.

You could also reduce your initial costs by narrating yourself or doing royalty share deals.

One of the advantages of independent publishing in any format is control of your intellectual property asset. You can take advantage of new distribution partners and marketing opportunities over time, which are emerging almost every month in this growth area.

Is it worth producing an audiobook?

You need to consider your budget when producing audio as an independent author as it is the most expensive format to create, especially if you have a long book or series and if you're using professional narration. These questions will help you to decide whether it's worth considering.

- Do you have an audience for your books already?

- Have you sold sufficient numbers of your ebooks or print books to indicate there will be sales for your audiobook?

- Do you have a budget for production and marketing? Have you estimated how long it will take to see a return on investment?

- Do you have a number of books you can produce in audio format, so customers have more to buy if they enjoy the first one?

- Do you have a way to market your audiobooks?

If you cannot answer yes to all these questions, you might consider waiting before investing in audio, or trying to license your audio rights.

How do you receive income from audiobooks as an independent?

If you use ACX, you receive payments 30 days after the end of the month of sale, so I receive my October royalties at the end of November. Findaway Voices and other audiobook distributors pay at the end of the month following when they are paid by the retailers. Your royalties will depend on the number of sales, borrows, credits used in subscription services, and checkouts from libraries.

You can also receive Bounty payments from Audible when new listeners sign up for the service and listen to your audiobook first. This is US$75 at the time of writing.

You can sell audiobooks through the Authors Direct app, which is available if you publish through Findaway Voices. This gives you access to BookBub's Chirp audiobook promotion site, and hopefully, this ecosystem will encourage direct sales. It is only available in specific countries but will no doubt expand over time.

You can also sell audiobook files directly through digital sites like Payhip or Shopify. You receive the money immediately through PayPal, but the customer has to get the files onto their device, so you may have more customer service issues. Plus, you will need to account for digital sales tax. Although most sites have a way to help process these payments, the tax will impact your revenue.

Audiobook listeners often buy in multiple formats

This benefit is rarely discussed, possibly because it's so difficult to track how readers buy through opaque ecosystems like Amazon. But anecdotal evidence suggests that audiobook readers buy in multiple formats, for example, print editions for notes or looking up resources later, or ebooks to get cheaper audio deals.

Amazon Matchmaker will search for audiobooks that match ebooks already purchased, so this implies there is a group of readers who behave like this.

Watch out for new opportunities

It's still the early days of the digital audiobook revolution, and new companies spring up all the time, as well as new possibilities emerging for promotions and marketing. If you control your worldwide audiobook rights, you can participate in new opportunities in the global market, expanding your reach and your revenue. We live in exciting times!

Questions:

- How does the money work if you license your rights?

- How does the money work if you independently publish?

- What are the pros and cons of each for your situation?

Part 2: Podcasting

2.1 Why podcasting is important for authors

Whether you want to host your own show or appear as a guest, podcasting is a fantastic opportunity for authors. Here are some of the reasons that you might consider it.

(1) Book marketing for a voice-first audience

As noted in the Introduction, I don't read blogs anymore and haven't done for years. I also ignore most marketing emails, so if you are only marketing your book through written media, you will not reach a reader like me. And I'm certainly not alone.

I consume content by listening to podcasts and audiobooks, and by reading books or watching documentaries and TV shows. I'm car-free so I spend a lot of time walking. If I'm alone, I'll listen to a podcast or a non-fiction book on 1.5x speed. If I want to learn something, I'll search my podcast app for that topic, then start listening straight away. If you're not marketing on audio, you are completely off my radar as a reader.

Discovery is also amplified by having audio available. Google announced in August 2019 that they would index podcast episodes (not just shows) and display them on the first page of results in a similar way they do with video.

You can stand out more easily in audio as there are millions of blogs and written articles on the internet, but far fewer podcast episodes.

(2) Reach an international market — and potentially more people than will read your books

My podcast reaches a larger market and helps more people than my books do. At the time of writing, *The Creative Penn Podcast* has had over four million downloads across 222 countries.

In comparison, I have not sold a million books (yet), and I have 'only' sold books in 136 countries, which is still pretty awesome, but nowhere near the reach of my podcast.

In terms of demographics, the US makes up 60% of downloads, with the UK, Australia, Canada, Germany and New Zealand coming in next — but there are also downloads from Japan and India, Korea, Brazil, Saudi Arabia, Israel and Iran among others. Creatives, we are a glorious United Nations of a show!

I used to want my books to be everything, but in this busy world, many people prefer to listen, or read with their ears, than to read with their eyes.

You can sometimes change someone's life more effectively through a podcast or an audiobook than through the written word, and that's OK.

(3) Build a trusted relationship with your audience and market without the hard sell

"There has to be some emotional anchor for the listener, someone they feel interested in, connected to, and invested in. It is someone that they would (occasionally) sacrifice other activities for just to hear from them, understand them, relate to them, and learn from them."

Eric Nuzum, Make Noise: A Creator's Guide to Podcasting and Great Audio Storytelling

We live in a world where trust is scarce, and consumers are increasingly rejecting mainstream media for more personal connection.

Podcasting is scalable one-to-one communication. Think about how a podcast works. You create audio, either on your own or in conversation with others, and then you put it out in the world.

Someone somewhere sometime downloads or streams that audio and immediately, you are in their head — maybe for minutes, maybe for hours.

That person listens to your voice and makes a judgment within seconds as to whether they want to keep listening. If they do, you will establish a trusted relationship over time, and people want to do business with people they know, like and trust. Some listeners will buy your books, products, and services because they have a connection.

I've been podcasting for over a decade, and listeners will often come up to me at events and say, "I feel like I know you." It is my voice over the internet that produces this relationship, because it's authentically me.

So, double down on being human. You are not a big brand. Flawed is OK.

> "Podcasting has definitely helped me establish a stronger connection with my readers, who are now an audience! I've had great feedback from people who have been on my mailing list for years, who tell me they feel they are getting to know me better and engaging with my ideas more by hearing my voice. Plus I'm reaching lots of new people, who hear the show first then start exploring my writing, on my blog, in my books, and via the free course I send out via email."

Mark McGuinness, The 21st Century Creative Podcast

(4) Build authority in your niche

Podcast interviews are a great way to establish your authority, and this can lead to many more opportunities, especially if your business model includes speaking, consulting or coaching. Most of my speaking opportunities over the last decade have come from the podcast, including trips to Bali, Florida, Zurich, Auckland and London.

Listeners will often consume multiple podcasts in a niche, and if they hear you on a number of shows over time, they will understand you have a level of knowledge and experience they can trust.

"Podcasting is the easiest way for an introvert to network. Best of all, it doesn't seem like networking. You're just blabbing to a co-host or a guest for an hour and uploading the file afterward. But after a couple of years of that, you might find you're pretty well-known in your industry and people reach out to you instead of the other way around."

Lindsay Buroker, co-host of the Six-Figure Author Podcast

(5) Establish relationships with influencers

I started podcasting because I felt isolated in my corner of the world, and I wanted to meet creative people. I have succeeded in that goal beyond anything I could have imagined, as I can pretty much go anywhere now and meet other independent creatives. I also met many of my friends in real life through the podcast and social media.

There are many people you cannot pay for consulting time, but if you invite them on a podcast, you can ask them questions for an hour. That's certainly true of me! I rarely do consulting, but I am more than happy to come on an established podcast and talk in public about what might help the host and their audience.

"Interviewing guests for my podcast is a great way to grow my professional network. Now, when I come across someone whose work I love, I can reach out to them and invite them on the show. It's a great way to help them by spreading the word about their work, and it's been the start of some great conversations and even friendships."

Mark McGuinness, The 21st Century Creative Podcast

(6) Build other streams of revenue

A podcast is not primarily about direct book sales income. Sure, you will sell more books over time as your audience grows, but there are also other ways for podcasting to bring in revenue.

Advertising is the primary method of monetization, with Patreon and direct sponsorship another significant stream.

You can also use it to sell products, services, or use affiliate marketing. If you use a transcript, text-based search will bring people to your site. Google started indexing podcast episodes in August 2019, so over time, voice search will bring traffic to your site. Many of those visitors will stay a while, and if you have useful, inspirational, or entertaining products or services, they may buy.

You can also use a call to action on your podcast, directing people to your show notes or to an email opt-in. I mention my *Author Blueprint* at the end of my show every week, so people know they can visit:

TheCreativePenn.com/blueprint to learn more.

There's more about the money side of podcasting in chapter 2.19.

Questions:

- Why is podcasting important for authors? What are some of the benefits that you find most interesting?

2.2 What's the difference between a podcast and an audiobook?

On the surface, there are many similarities between podcasts and audiobooks, especially in a digital world where both are audio files downloaded onto a portable device. But while the distribution method may be similar, audiobooks and podcasts are quite different in terms of how they are created, how the listener treats them, and how the revenue model works.

An audiobook is a recording of a specific written text — either a book, a play, or something written specifically for audio, but it starts with written text turned into an audio format. It is self-contained and has a clear beginning and end.

Listeners will usually download a complete audiobook from a retailer, paying through subscription or direct purchase, similar to book sales in other formats.

A podcast is usually episodic and works more like a radio show. It is created primarily for the audio format and might be an unscripted conversation, an interview, or a presented show. Some podcasts have transcripts produced, but most exist only in audio.

Listeners subscribe for free through podcast apps on mobile devices, smart speakers, or in-car players. Episodes are downloaded automatically once a listener has subscribed, although some podcast apps will pause downloads if the listener hasn't accessed the show for a while.

The revenue model is through advertising, patronage, or sales and marketing for a wider business, although some podcast hosts are also trying premium subscriptions.

2.3 Types of podcasts

"Podcasting is the generous act of showing up,
earning trust and authority because you care
enough to raise your hand and speak up."

Seth Godin

There are many different kinds of podcasts. This chapter
is a brief overview, so you get a broad idea of what might
interest you as a listener, but also what you could utilize as
an author.

Seasonal or episodic

Most podcasts are episodic — for example, *The Creative
Penn Podcast*, my weekly show, goes out every Monday
morning. I've been podcasting since 2009 and have had
a regular schedule for over a decade. My other show, the
Books and Travel Podcast, is bi-monthly, coming out every
other Thursday.

Seasonal podcasts are usually around specific topics and
may involve higher production value and more in-depth
research. For example, *Sleepwalkers* is a fantastic show
about the impact of AI on society. It uses multiple interviews combined into a narrative flow on a specific topic per
episode for a limited season.

Seasonal shows can also work well when the host has lots
of other work and can't commit to an ongoing production
schedule. The *Writing Excuses Podcast* is well-known in

the writing community. The authors involved are all professionals and need time to work on their books, so the seasonal format works well for the hosts.

Some seasonal shows have an overlap with audiobooks — for example, the award-winning podcast, *Serial,* tells one story end to end over the course of a season. Some authors release audio fiction and even whole audiobooks through podcast networks.

Talk show with interviews

These can be solo or with regular co-hosts. Some of the most popular podcasts are this format, for example, *The Joe Rogan Experience*, or in the author niche, my show, *The Creative Penn Podcast.*

The host or co-hosts are the anchors, and different guests come on the show to discuss specific topics. There are various segments to the program, one of which may be a personal update from the host or co-hosts which gives the audience a reason to come back next week.

Teaching or presentation

A good example of a teaching show is Dan Carlin's *Hardcore History*, which tackles great swathes of history over epic seasons where individual episodes can last for several hours each.

TED Talks also have several podcasts, some with replays of original talks, and others that gather several speakers into one topic show.

I sometimes do solo shows on specific topics, for example, 9 Ways that Artificial Intelligence will Disrupt Authors and Publishing in the Next Decade on *The Creative Penn Podcast*; or Escape, Reinvention, Curiosity, Challenge. Why Travel? on *Books and Travel*. These take a lot more time than interviews in terms of preparation and production.

Highly produced, scripted shows

While the previous examples can be done easily by independent producers with little to no budget, there are now a lot of different shows funded by professional networks with investment in top journalists, presenters, and sound production.

Each episode will be highly scripted and produced by a team of professionals. For example, Wondery's *Dirty John,* which was turned into a TV show, or *This American Life*, one of the most popular podcasts in the world with five million listeners every week.

Podcast fiction

Humans have always told stories around the campfire, and podcast fiction is just the latest iteration of this idea. It's an incredibly creative, vibrant, and diverse niche where storytellers, voice talent, and producers combine to create everything from short stories read by the author every week to full-cast audio productions set in fictional worlds.

I started listening to podcast fiction back in 2007 when Podiobooks (now Scribl.com) provided a way for authors to get their audiobooks into the world before podcasting went mainstream and before audiobooks went digital. I binge-listened to *7th Son* by JC Hutchins and Scott Sigler's *Infected*, authors who went on to get book deals with mainstream publishers after their audio-first success.

Podcast fiction hit the mainstream with *Welcome to Night Vale* in 2012. The show features community updates from a small desert town where conspiracy theories have come to life. It now has an accompanying book series, a whole range of merchandise, and even live shows with the performers.

* * *

These are just the main types of shows, but podcasting continues to expand. There are opportunities for independent creators in all niches, as well as possibilities for journalists, freelance writers, and voice talent with the networks that continue to invest in the podcast space.

Questions:

- What are the different types of podcasts?

- Try a few episodes of each, so you understand the possibilities. What do you like or dislike about the different types?

2.4 How to research and pitch podcasters

Now you've decided that you want to appear on podcasts, how do you approach the right shows?

(1) Identify your niche

Whether you want to get interviews on other people's podcasts or start your own show, you need to know your niche and where it might intersect with shows already out there. Consider these questions:

What's your book about?

This is easy for non-fiction authors as it's the **topic of your book**. For this book, I could pitch podcasts in the podcasting niche (very meta), as well as podcasts for voice artists, authors, and perhaps even some in the voice technology space.

But this question has two levels for fiction authors.

You can pitch podcasts in your genre. For example, my ARKANE novels are 'Dan Brown meets Lara Croft,' action-adventure, conspiracy thrillers where secret agents travel around the world solving supernatural mysteries. But fiction interview podcasts are not a big niche, and they rarely last long because of limited monetization potential. I can also go on writing podcasts and talk about my writing process, but again, this is not a large niche.

So I recommend you widen your scope by considering the **themes that underlie your stories as well as settings**. These are often wide-ranging and give you more opportunity for interviews on podcasts with larger audiences. For example, I could pitch podcasts about travel, religion, psychology, conspiracies, creativity, and more. These shows also have the benefit of reaching a wider audience than just the writing community, so dig deep into the various layers of your work to find target shows.

Who are you?

I recently talked to a non-fiction author writing in the entrepreneurship niche. She had clear goals around pitching popular entrepreneurial podcasts, but these are really over-subscribed and often booked well in advance, and she might not stand out in a sea of similar guests.

But she is also a British female entrepreneur, a working mother of two young children, a survivor of a health crisis that almost took her life, a long-distance runner, and a dog-lover.

These aspects of her personality are tangential to the topic of her book, but they could also take her message into other niches where she can reach a totally new audience. Think about yourself in the same way.

(2) Start listening to podcasts

If you don't already listen to podcasts, it's time to start. You need to understand how the format works and get used to the way different hosts interact.

The easiest way to find shows is to open a podcast app on your phone — there are many options, but they all work the same way. Try Apple Podcasts, Google Podcasts, Spotify or Stitcher if you don't know where to start.

You can find recommendations by niche, and you can also use the search bar to find specific episodes. If I'm interested in a topic, I will search on the podcast app, then download episodes that sound interesting without subscribing to the shows. In this way, I try different voices without committing. I might delete the show within a few minutes, or continue listening to any that resonate.

As you listen to your chosen show, consider what you like and what you don't like. What holds your attention? What makes you skip forward or stop listening altogether? What's the interview style? How is the podcast making money?

You can also find podcasts by doing a Google search on "Top podcasts for dog-lovers" or whatever your niche is. You can limit this to the last year to see recent shows. You can also Google other authors in your niche to see what shows they've been on, for example, "Joanna Penn + podcast interview" will bring up some of my backlist.

(3) Identify appropriate shows and research the host and audience

When you find a podcast that you'd like to pitch, investigate it further. Keep a spreadsheet or document so you can track who you interact with over time.

Note the name of the host and any key points that you have in common. Think about your pitch from the host's point of view. What will be useful and valuable for their audience? What can you offer that would be great content for them? Why would you make a good guest?

Essentially, **you are asking to go into the host's house and talk to an audience they have worked hard, possibly over years, to cultivate.** Play by their rules and don't take the opportunity for granted.

Of course, the very best way to get on a show is by invitation from the host. This can happen if you develop a relationship over time. It may be that you attend an event with them, or help them with something, or you can start by connecting through social media. Follow the host and the podcast, share quotes, and comment on the episode if appropriate. Obviously, don't be a stalker, but cultivating long-term relationships is the best way to connect.

(4) Pitch in reverse order of importance

Make a list of the podcasts you'd like to appear on. Rank them according to audience size, the level of the guests and how many episodes they have, as well as how likely you are to get on the show.

There are hierarchies in every industry and we all have to start at the bottom. Don't pitch for a top-rated show if you are just starting out and you have no experience. You need practice anyway, so start with smaller shows that may be less established with fewer episodes. You don't want your first ever podcast to be the biggest one in your niche!

Send your pitch to the shows at the bottom of your list first — although, of course, you don't need to tell them that!

If they say yes, fantastic. Be ready to interview and give 150% value.

If the podcaster doesn't reply, or rejects you, don't worry, this is normal. Like anything, you will never get 100% acceptance. You might need to refine your pitch, or the podcast just isn't right for you at this time. It's worth pitching again in the future once you have more experience. I've had people on *The Creative Penn Podcast* many years after they first pitched me. They weren't appropriate when they first started out, but over time, they proved themselves, stood out from the pack and came on the show with something valuable to share.

(5) Craft your pitch email

Once you've decided on a podcast, craft a personal pitch email with the following essential inclusions.

A personal greeting that makes it clear you know who the host is and that you have listened to the show. You could mention a specific episode or two and why you thought they were particularly useful. Remember, podcast hosts get these pitches every day, so don't make it up or use language that demonstrates you haven't even listened. Trust me, it's easy to tell!

A topic (or several) that would be useful to the audience that makes it clear you have done your homework around what would be valuable.

Your credentials and why you are a good person to speak on this topic. Presumably you have a book on it, but this might also mean your personal experience. Include links to your website, social media, your book, and any other ways that you can be verified.

Make sure your website is ready. If a pitch makes it through my assistant, the first thing I do is go to the person's website and have a look around. Make sure your bio is up to date, your links to social media actually work, and that your books are listed and linked.

Example of a bad pitch

> Hi Joanna,
>
> I am working on self-publishing my first romance book and I'd like to be on your show. Please let me know when I can be interviewed.

I get this type of email almost every day and it is a terrible pitch.

This person has clearly not listened to my show because they would know I don't interview authors who are just starting out. There is no consideration for my audience. The author thinks that publishing a book is reason enough to be interviewed, and the arrogant tone of the email assumes that they will be accepted.

This type of pitch receives a form rejection from my assistant, but hopefully, you can see that it's easy to do much better than that with even a little bit of research upfront.

Here are two examples of perfect pitches, one non-fiction and one fiction, so that you can see the possibilities.

Example of a perfect pitch for
The Creative Penn Podcast

Hi, Joanna,

I'm hoping you'll consider a future podcast episode covering the topic of my latest non-fiction book, inspired in part by your book, *The Healthy Writer*.

The premise of *Happiness, Anxiety, and Writing: Using Your Creativity To Live A Calmer, Happier Life* is that for a lot of writers, the imagination and skills key to writing also can cause or increase anxiety. For example, asking *What If* and imagining the worst possible outcome is great for creating strong plots but can be destructive in our personal lives.

The book shares clear, simple steps for using our writers' minds in new ways to create calm and happiness. It's part How To, part memoir drawn from my own decade of living with and overcoming anxiety.

If you think it might be helpful to your listeners, I hope you'll consider me as a guest. The content is evergreen, so it could fit in any time. And while I haven't been on a podcast before, I'm experienced at public speaking and interviews through my legal career.

Here's a link to an ARC for the book if you'd like to check out a few pages before deciding.

Thanks so much for considering my request. And for all the great content you share!

Lisa
Lisa M. Lilly
LisaLilly.com

* * *

This is a perfect pitch in every way. It is clear that Lisa knows me, my books, and my audience, and she offers enough detail so I can clearly see the arc of an episode. She includes links to her website and a link to a downloadable copy of her book. She is honest about her experience and is flexible on timing.

Even though she didn't mention it, I have met Lisa at several writing conferences, and she's also a Patron of the podcast, so I know her name. It doesn't guarantee her an interview, but it adds to the overall weight.

> I booked Lisa for a show on Happiness, Anxiety and Writing, and she was fantastic. You can listen at TheCreativePenn.com/lisa

Example of a perfect pitch for Books and Travel

> Hi Jo,
>
> I know and love your work from your Creative Penn podcasts, books and articles. I've reached out to you a few times, and always appreciated the time you have taken to respond.
>
> So my pitch for a potential interview is this: GREEN-LAND.
>
> More specifically: living and working in an 'exotic' location that has inspired my writing, and allowed me to make a living as an indie writer.
>
> And the longer explanation:

I have pursued the Arctic in literature and travel since reading Jack London stories with a torch beneath the bedsheets as a teenager, all the way to working in Greenland as an adult.

I lived and worked as a teacher in subsistence hunting communities for 6 years in Greenland before moving to the capital, Nuuk, for my 7th year.

While in Greenland, I had a team of 13 sledge dogs, running on the sea ice for three years. And I spent a month on a solo kayak expedition, paddling alongside whales and icebergs under the midnight sun. That particular experience — traveling solo in the wilderness — was profound. I read *Game of Thrones* on that trip — very surreal!

Travel and living abroad (I am originally English but publish under a Danish name) has shaped me, my stories, and my life. I am super interested in all things Arctic, and would love to share stories of strange things I have eaten, amazing wildlife and nature experiences, and my deep respect for the Greenlandic people and their culture. All these things shape my writing.

I've dreamed about what I might say if I ever got the chance to be interviewed for your *Creative Penn Podcast*. However, I feel your *Books and Travel Podcast* is perhaps more relevant for me. Please let me know if you think so, too.

If not, no worries, I'll just look forward to your next podcast — across all your platforms!

Thanks. :-)
Christoffer
Christoffer-Petersen.com

* * *

This perfect pitch demonstrates a real understanding of my podcast audience with a well-crafted email that gives an insight into the author and an outline for an interview. I use the name 'Jo' for my *Books and Travel Podcast* so that personalization makes it clear that he listens.

> I booked Christoffer for a show about Greenland, and we talked about his novels set in the Arctic. It's a great example of choosing a tangential podcast for a novelist. You can listen at:

> BooksAndTravel.page/greenland

Questions:

- What potential niches could you target for your book? Think topics, theme, settings and your own interests.

- What shows do you currently listen to that resonate with your topic?

- Make a list of 15-20 other podcasts you could pitch in your niche and list them in order of importance

- Find out about each host and their audience. What can you offer that would be useful?

- Craft your first pitch for a podcast interview. Does it follow the recommendations as outlined?

- How will you deal with success or rejection?

2.5 How to be a great podcast guest

You've been booked for a show — congratulations!

These tips will help you make it the best experience for the audience, the host, and also for you.

(1) Research the host and the audience

You should already know about the show, especially if you pitched for the interview. Still, it's worth spending more time listening to episodes and noting down anything useful about the host or the audience so you can serve them in the best way you can. The more useful you are, the more inspiring or entertaining, the more they are likely to care about you and be interested in your book. Podcasts can be fantastic word-of-mouth marketing, so you need to make a good impression.

Make sure you write down the name of the host and any key points on a piece of paper next to you so you can refer to it easily. Have they written a book or something you should know about? Or maybe they have something in their bio that shows you have an interest in common.

I always like to find out where people live, not just for time zone reasons, but because it tells you a lot about their life. I will also check out their Twitter stream or other social media on the day of the interview to see if there is any new information they haven't yet added to their website.

In terms of the audience, try to understand what level they are within your niche. For example, I do many interviews about writing books, but it is a different conversation when speaking to a podcast for accountants on writing a book for their business than it is to a podcast for established thriller writers. If you know who you're talking to, you can tailor your material in a much more effective way.

Weave these nuggets into the conversation naturally. It shows that you have done your homework, and podcast hosts love that.

(2) Check your technology and prepare your environment beforehand

Most podcast interviews are conducted over the internet, so you will be sent a link to join at the appropriate time. The most common services at the time of writing are Skype, Zoom, Zencastr, and CleanFeed, and all require different setups.

If you're using new technology, test it first with a friend to make sure your device is properly set up. If you have used the software before, it may still need updating, so log on early or the day before to check the settings.

It can be disconcerting if you turn up for an interview and then can't get the tech to work. You will feel bad. The host may be annoyed. You can try to rearrange, but you may lose the opportunity altogether, so be prepared.

Check your internet connection, especially if you're using video as it requires significant bandwidth. If possible, make sure you're on wired internet instead of Wi-Fi, and if you are on Wi-Fi, make sure you've got a good signal. Close down any other programs and make sure others in your house are not downloading huge files that might impact internet speed.

If you're planning to do a lot of interviews, it's worth investing in a separate stand-alone microphone and use earbuds to separate input and output channels for better sound quality. I use a Blue Yeti microphone, and my Apple iPhone earbuds plugged into the laptop. If you don't have a separate microphone, it's still worth using earbuds — phone headset ones are usually fine — so the output audio doesn't echo around the room. You can also use a pop filter over the microphone to stop plosive sounds. The more you record, the more you discover your voice issues, covered in detail in chapter 1.7 on audiobook narration, where the tips are just as applicable to podcasting.

As a host, I will always do a sound check with my guests before hitting Record, but if you are ready, you will make a good impression and look like a professional.

If you haven't done interviews in a specific location before, check the sound quality of the room space. Hard floors and high ceilings may cause an echo, so somewhere with soft furnishings is a better idea, or purchase some sound blankets. This is why so many people podcast in a closet!

Make sure children and animals are elsewhere. Turn off your phone. Put a Do Not Disturb sign on your door if there are other people in the house.

If this is an important interview and things are difficult to arrange at home, it's worth hiring a room at a co-working space, then make sure you have a time buffer so you can set everything up beforehand.

Have a glass of room temperature water nearby as you might get a dry mouth if you're nervous. During the interview, sip water while the host is talking, and try not to slurp. Remember, it's a conversation, so you will be able to take breaks as they respond and interact. If you have no time for a sip of water, you are performing a monologue. Stop already!

(3) Respect the clock

Interviews are arranged for a particular time slot, and you should get an automated reminder if you have booked using calendar software. If you don't use an online calendar, then make sure you have checked the time well in advance, especially if the host is in another time zone. Make sure to allow some extra time in case the interview over-runs or you are late starting.

Most interviews I do are with people in other countries, so I am always obsessively checking the time in their city before the interview. This is particularly important around the switch to and from daylight savings time between the US and Europe as there are a couple of weeks when the time difference is not the same as usual.

Be on time or a few minutes early for the meeting. If the host is not there by five minutes past, then check your email as they might have messaged about a delay.

During the interview, be aware of time passing so you can be sure to have a conversation and not just go off into a mono-logue on a topic. Experienced podcast hosts will control time through interruption, so they get their questions answered, but it's good to be aware of how fast time flies.

Most podcast hosts will keep to time so you can expect to wind up with a few minutes to spare. But sometimes, they might go over. It's hard to interrupt the flow of an interview when you're the guest, but if you do have to leave, use gentle reminders like, "I know we're coming to the end of the time now, so I'll keep this short."

(4) It's not about you. It's about the audience.

It's natural to be nervous before an interview, but don't worry. It's not about you, it's about the audience. Most listeners won't even know who you are at the beginning of the show. They just want information, inspiration or entertainment depending on the genre.

> Maya Angelou said it best: "People will forget what you said. People will forget what you did. But people will never forget how you made them feel."

Your energy is incredibly important, and how you interact with the host, how you are as a real person, will resonate far more than what you say. We all crave authentic connection, and that is clear in someone's voice.

I'm an introvert, and I know it can be hard to bring the energy sometimes, especially when I'm doing an interview at the end of a long day and I'm tired. But the audience is listening in another time in another place, so you need to bring your energy to the show.

Try listening to some upbeat music beforehand, move your body, reset your intentions. Maybe even pour yourself a gin and tonic, my favorite energy booster for interviews after

6 pm! Do whatever it takes to serve the audience because you never know where this opportunity might lead.

(5) Go with the flow

A podcast interview should be a natural conversation. The host may send questions in advance, but only ever prepare bullet points. Never read from your notes, as it is immediately apparent in the way your voice changes. You want to connect with the host on the line and the people listening.

You know more than you think, so prepare as much as possible and then relax into the interview. I know this is hard. The first time I went on live radio back in 2008, I had ten pages of notes spread out around me, so I had a backup if I just blanked on the phone. It went well, and I was only on for a few minutes anyway. I still prep for interviews as much as possible, but I don't look at my notes during the conversation, and it usually changes direction anyway.

You are the expert on your book. You know your story. You know your niche. Trust yourself to bring that out in the moment.

Make your answers personal, share your stories, and don't just spout catchphrases from your book. In fact, mention your book as little as possible. Let the host do it as part of the intro, and you'll likely get a chance to mention it at the end. Never answer a question with, "In my book it says …" Just answer the question in a way that will best serve the audience. Be as generous as you can with your answers, and that energy will attract people to you and make them *want* to buy your book.

Most importantly, **this is a conversation, not a monologue**.

Don't go on too long answering one question. On the other hand, don't be too short. One of the worst interviewees I ever had was practically monosyllabic. I had to work so hard to make it a decent conversation.

You can ask questions, too. Bring the host into the conversation. Make it interactive. Listen to their replies and respond appropriately, even if the topic wasn't on the proposed agenda. Good interviewers don't just read a list of questions. They go where curiosity takes them, so be prepared to change tack or go deeper into a topic.

Have a pen and paper nearby in case you think of things you want to bring up during the interview. I often write down words or notes so that I can circle back to a topic using the same language that the host used earlier. This makes the interview more natural.

Toward the end of the interview, the podcast host will ask you where people can find you and your book/s. Prepare your call to action and remember that you are on audio.

Make it short and specific and use easy to remember links. Make it evergreen, as many listeners will find the show weeks, months, or even years later.

My call to action for my Joanna Penn brand is:

> "My books are available on all the usual online retail stores — and if you'd like to hear more about writing, join me on *The Creative Penn Podcast*, or TheCreativePenn.com, and that's Penn with a double 'n.' If you have a question, find me on Twitter @thecreativepenn."

Note that my call to action is primarily for another podcast because this is an audio-first environment. You might not have a podcast, but you should at least have a website with an easy-to-say link. Don't spout all your social media profiles and sites. Listeners know how to google and how to find books online. If they're interested in you, they will find your info or go to the podcast show notes. Just be succinct so the host can say thanks and goodbye.

(6) Follow up and promote the show

Most podcast hosts will record well in advance and will let you know when the episode goes live. Promote the link if appropriate, and thank the host by email or by sharing on social media. They will see it if you tag them.

Some episodes I've promoted on other shows have ended up being shared again by that host because I've directed so much traffic to it. Hosts certainly appreciate the effort and will continue to promote popular episodes, so you can get ongoing marketing this way.

What if the interview goes badly?

There are several ways that an interview can go wrong.

Tech issues are the most common, but podcast hosts are used to this. If the internet won't work, or you get cut off, or the recording failed, don't worry. You will likely just rearrange for another day. Be apologetic if it's your fault and understanding if it's not, and make the second time even better.

Lack of research on either side can also be an issue. I've been on shows where the host has asked me about things I have no experience of. At other times, I've pronounced the host's name wrong, or misunderstood what they asked.

On one occasion, the host kept trying to catch me out with nasty questions and our rapport was non-existent. I wish I had cut the call short and asked for the interview not to be aired. It went out, and I probably sounded like an idiot, but I decided to ignore it and move on.

But these experiences are rare. I've done over six hundred interviews in the last decade, and most have been brilliant.

Everything gets better with practice. There will inevitably be issues, but these things happen, and you can't let them stop you trying again. Prepare as much as possible, give it your best and see what happens.

* * *

Questions:

- Have you researched the host and audience? Do you know how best to serve them?

- Have you prepared your technical setup and environment for the best recording experience?

- Have you prepared talking points?

- How will you ensure that the audience remembers how you made them feel?

- How will you make sure that you can bring your energy?

- How will you make sure the conversation is natural?

- What is your call to action? Have you said it out loud to check that your link is easy to say?

- What will you do after the interview?

- What if the interview goes badly? How will you make sure it's better next time?

2.6 Should you start your own podcast?

"Podcasting is the new blogging. Not as a way
to make big dollars (blogging didn't do that either).
But as a way to share your ideas, to lead your
community, to earn trust."

Seth Godin

Podcasting is a great way to reach an audience through an authentic, personalized medium, but not every author should start a podcast, in the same way that not every author should start a blog.

The reality is that most podcasts, like most blogs, disappear over time. 'Podfade' is the industry term for shows that launch, publish a few episodes and then disappear because it's too much work, life gets in the way, or interests change.

If you're thinking about starting your own show, consider the following questions.

What is your why?

There can be money in podcasting once you have an established audience, but there is no point in starting a show for income reasons alone. The podcast will take a lot of time and effort on your part, as well as money for equipment and potentially hosting. It may take years to show a financial return on investment. It certainly took that long for me.

So what is a good reason to start your own show?

I started podcasting because I had no author friends, no way to find a community in the days before being an independent author was acceptable. I lived in Brisbane, Australia, back in 2008, and I knew that there was a community of indie authors in the US. I couldn't meet them in person, so I decided to start an interview show. It was still the early days of podcasting, so almost everyone I asked said yes, and slowly, I built up a network of creative people who at least knew I existed. Some of those people are my friends in real life many years later.

Podcasting is now a valuable income stream for my business, but I started as a way to network with other creators, and it still serves that purpose, plus I enjoy sharing curated updates on the publishing industry every week. *The Creative Penn Podcast* is a community, and I have met many listeners in person over the years. I've also learned a lot and expanded my skills and confidence along the way.

Here are some other podcasters on why they keep creating.

"For me, podcasting isn't about marketing or selling more books. It allows me an opportunity to continue to learn and grow my knowledge about the industry and related technologies … It also allows me an authentic way to connect with movers, shakers, thinkers, and doers … and connect with listeners and the greater writing community."

Mark Leslie Lefebvre, Stark Reflections on Writing and Publishing, StarkReflections.ca

"I started podcasting in order to help myself: I wanted to know other writers' processes because I felt my own writing process was subpar and could use some help. Immediately I learned two things: first, my writing process — as clunky as it is — is just fine, and second, the thing I love best about podcasting is helping others.

But the main delight of podcasting is that it helps me be a better human. That sounds a bit too grand, maybe, but it's true. I encourage others to attempt their truest, deepest calling, and in doing so, I am repaid tenfold with the joy it brings me.

Every time I think of giving it up (which I do, as time becomes more and more hard to find), I imagine my life without podcasting, and life loses some color. It's a way to give back, which to me is crucial for my overall mental health and happiness."

Rachael Herron, Author and Podcaster
RachaelHerron.com

Are you ready to learn?

Podcasting requires learning new technical skills around microphones and audio software as well as discovering new websites for distribution, new language around voice technologies, and new marketing techniques. You will also need to learn personal skills around interviewing or being interviewed.

You can learn all of this — as you can learn any skill — but you need the right attitude to get through the inevitable technical hurdles, as well as the extra time and budget that will be required.

Are you ready to put yourself out there?

As a podcaster, you are often alone when speaking into a microphone, in the same way that an author is alone at the keyboard, but the result of that time alone will go out into the world, and other people will listen at some point. They will get to hear your thoughts — and yes, they will judge you, and that can be terrifying!

It was years before I shared anything personal on *The Creative Penn Podcast*. I thought the people I interviewed were incredible and that listeners only wanted to learn from them, but over time, I discovered that the host is the anchor. Many listeners remain loyal to a show because they follow the host's journey over time. So, you need to bring your personal side, you need to share openly, if you want people to keep coming back. I know it's hard, but if you want to host a successful podcast, it's about personal branding, and connecting with listeners by sharing your authentic voice.

Who is your show for?
What's in it for them?

Podcasting has to be all about the listener, or there's no point in publishing your audio to the world. In the same way, if you write a personal journal with no thought to the reader, then don't bother publishing a book.

What value do you provide? What transformation will a listener go through?

This is important because **segmentation is everything** with podcasting, even more so than the topics you cover. I listen to a lot of podcast episodes for the specific topic but I might not subscribe or revisit the show, whereas if I gel with a podcast host, I'll subscribe and keep coming back.

As with our writing, it's better to be podcasting within a niche you know intimately and love because your listener avatar is you. I've been podcasting at *The Creative Penn* for over a decade because it's about the author journey, and I'm still on the path myself. I ask the right questions because they are my questions, too. I face the same fears, and I know the ups and downs of the creative rollercoaster.

So, who is your show for, and why will people keep coming back?

Is your niche big enough to justify your time?

This is difficult to judge and will depend on why you're podcasting. If there are shows in the niche already, chances are that there is a big enough audience. If you can come up with at least ten other podcasts in your niche, then it's already maturing.

However, in saying that, when I started *The Creative Penn Podcast*, there were no other shows for independent authors. There were some writing podcasts — *Writing Excuses* and *I Should Be Writing* — but they were not about independent creators or making a living writing. It was the very early days of what became a movement, and I had no idea what it would become. I was early in the niche, and it paid off, so that might be your situation as well.

The niche may start small, but it might grow. This may be true because of the topic, for example, vegan health has exploded in the last few years. Some early podcasters and bloggers in that niche are doing very well now.

This may also be true in terms of demographics. At Frankfurt Book Fair Audio Summit in 2019, one speaker noted that Spanish language podcasts and audiobooks in Latin America are only just starting to take off and the companies involved are struggling to create content fast enough. I also met a podcaster from India who said that people haven't discovered podcasting there yet, but he is positioning himself for when they do, expecting huge returns down the line.

So, if you're early, hang in there!

Can you be consistent with your production?

It's not worth starting your own show unless you have enough time to produce consistently. Podcasting doesn't work if it's sporadic. You need to commit to a regular schedule, for example, weekly or bi-monthly, or create a seasonal show. If you podcast on an ad-hoc schedule when you 'feel' like it, you will lose momentum, and your listeners will find someone else to follow. You have to commit.

Is it too late to start a podcast?

Some people say that it's hard to start podcasting now there are so many shows, but luckily, you are an author, so you understand the same applies to any kind of art!

There are so many love stories in the world, is it worth writing another one? Of course it is, because no one has written the story that is in your mind with your unique point of view. The same is true with podcasting. You are unique, and no one has your voice and your experience.

We all have different lives, and we all bring a different perspective to the medium of podcasting. *The Creative Penn Podcast* is for independent authors who want to make a living with their writing. There are other podcasts in this niche (although I was one of the first!), but no one else has my unique experience — and no one else has yours.

You could also start a podcast for indie authors, but it would be nothing like mine. We could interview the same person or talk on the same topic, and we'd still have different shows. In the same way, we could both be given the same writing prompt in the same genre, and both write different books.

So no, it's not too late to start a podcast, especially if there isn't a show that represents your world view. Could *you* be that voice?

There's also the aspect of churn. Most podcasts — like most blogs and like most authors — disappear. The artist moves onto other things because it didn't turn out how they expected or the project finished. That's completely normal, and it means there is always room for new voices.

Is podcasting worth it?

For me, the answer is yes. Podcasting is the backbone of my non-fiction business, bringing me direct income as well as marketing my books. It also attracts a community of like-minded independent creatives, and I've found friends and colleagues all over the world through the interviews I've done over the years.

I have direct, intimate access to an audience with over four million downloads of my show across 222 countries. I help people with information and inspire authors to take control of their careers.

Podcasting is part of my creative body of work, in some cases, touching far more people through the spoken word than I have done with my written work.

Of course, I didn't know it would turn out this way in the early years of few listeners and a lot of work for little return. But now, I believe that podcasting is one of the best things I have done as a creative entrepreneur. If you choose to start your own show, persist longer than your peers, and you may well reap the rewards.

"Start thinking of yourself as someone who creates audio experiences that accompany listeners through their life, regardless of the platform it appears on."

Eric Nuzum, Make Noise: A Creator's Guide to Podcasting and Great Audio Storytelling

Questions:

- What is your why?

- Are you ready to learn new skills? Do you have the time and budget?

- Are you prepared to put yourself out there?

- Who is the show for? What's in it for them?

- Is the niche big enough? Is there potential future growth in your niche or demographic? What evidence do you have for thinking that way?

- Can you be consistent with production?

- What would make podcasting worth it for you?

2.7 Podcast prerequisites

I know you're keen to start recording, but there are a few things that you need to decide before you get into content creation.

(1) Know your market

What are the current big shows in your niche? What are some of the smaller shows? Have you listened to at least ten different podcasts in your potential niche and noted what you like and don't like about their content.

What specific audience are you going to serve? What do they want to know? How are you already part of that community?

(2) What is your definition of success?

If you know what you want to achieve, you are more likely to make that happen. For example, if your goal is to sell more books, you need to have a specific call to action about where to buy, and your show should relate to that content.

If you want to attract advertising revenue, it's a good idea to have target companies in mind and specific download numbers you want to hit before pitching them.

If you want to build a network in your niche, identify the top people you want to interview and research how you might reach them.

I always create for the long term, so my podcasts must offer immediate benefits through creative expression and networking, but also must pay their way eventually to at least offset the running costs. I monetized *The Creative Penn Podcast* after six years and have a three-year plan for *Books and Travel*, but for me, success in podcasting is more about serving my community and fulfilling a creative goal.

(3) Decide on the format of your show

Chapter 2.3 outlined the different types of shows that you might consider, but at some point, you have to decide what you are going to create.

How long will the show be? Consistency is key, so don't have ten minutes each for the first six weeks and then suddenly several two-hour shows. Any length can work, but you need to be consistent.

How often will it go out? Again, be consistent with your frequency because you want your show to become a habit. If I don't post an episode of *The Creative Penn* by 7 am UK time on a Monday, I get emails and tweets from concerned listeners. *Books and Travel* is every second Thursday.

Think about the time and technical skill you have available as well as what you want to achieve. For example, I love listening to high-production-value shows like *Sleepwalkers,* which has multiple interview guests and is highly scripted. But shows like that have corporate funding and a team of researchers and sound producers. I can't compete with them as an independent creator. I don't have the time or resources, so I choose an interview format with occasional solo episodes on specific topics, which is much easier to produce regularly, and consistency over time is key to growing a podcast audience.

You also need to **know yourself.** I much prefer to work alone as a creator, so I have never even tried to co-host a podcast. You might be the opposite. Choose what works for your personality type.

(4) Decide on the title of your show

Research podcasts in your niche and note the keywords used in their title, sub-title, and show notes. There are personality-based podcasts that include the name of the host, for example, *The Joe Rogan Experience*, and also keyword-rich shows that focus on being found in the search engines, for example, *The Social Media Marketing Podcast*.

Don't be too clever unless you also use a clear sub-title with obvious keywords. It's similar to non-fiction book titles. You want people to find you when they search for the niche they're interested in.

I started *The Creative Penn Podcast* before podcasting went mainstream so, to be honest, I didn't think too hard about the title of the show. But TheCreativePenn.com was my third website, and I did consider the name of my business for a long time before starting it. It includes my name (which is really Penn!) and the word 'creative,' so it fits my niche from a search engine perspective but also from a personality brand angle.

I thought about a second show for almost 18 months before starting *Books And Travel* in March 2019. I came up with lots of different titles, bought way too many domain names, and even built two other websites and recorded some episodes — but those fell by the wayside as I realized they would not work long term. When I finally settled on *Books and Travel*, it felt like the right choice. It's big enough in scope to encompass many of things I want to achieve, and it has the right keywords to attract a like-minded audience.

You also need a description for your show. You want to attract a target audience but also include keywords that resonate with your niche. The description for *The Creative Penn Podcast* is Interviews, Information and Inspiration on Writing, Publishing, Book Marketing, and Making a Living with your Writing.

(5) Decide on your podcast artwork

Every show needs an associated image. Podcast art is square, and if you have a business brand already, then incorporate that somehow. If you're starting from scratch, then look at other podcasts in your niche for ideas. Most have large type in some form, so it is easily readable on mobile devices.

If you are creating your own art, make sure you use **images from Royalty-Free sites** and be clear on permissions and rights licensing. If you have a logo designed, make sure copyright is assigned. Check your contracts with designers. More on intellectual property considerations in chapter 2.8.

Some podcasters use their image on the show art, which can be good for personal branding. I used to use my company logo but changed the art to feature my smiling face a few years back as *The Creative Penn* is a personality-based show.

My *Books and Travel Podcast* is a logo with large typography so it can be clearly read on mobile.

(6) Make an initial content plan

Podcasting is about regular, consistent production of audio content, so you need a constant flow of ideas. It's good to start thinking about this before you hit Record so that you know you will have enough content. Most podcasts launch with several episodes, so you'll need at least 5-10 to get started.

I plan my content on Google Sheets, which I share with my audio producer and my virtual assistant. *The Creative Penn Podcast* is usually planned 4-6 months in advance.

If your content is evergreen, you can record well ahead of time. I batch my interviews for both my podcasts and record the introductions closer to the live date.

Questions:

- Do you know your market? What are the top shows in your niche? What are the second-tier shows? What do you like and dislike about them?

- What specific audience are you going to serve? What do they want to know? How do you already fit into that community?

- What will the name of your show be? What ideas do you have for your sub-title and description?

- How long will the show be? How often will you publish?

- Have you organized your artwork?

- Have you made an initial content plan? Do you have enough ideas for an ongoing show?

2.8 Intellectual property considerations for podcasts

Many podcasters jump straight into creating audio without considering the possible intellectual property elements of podcasting. But it's important to respect the other creators involved at every stage of the process, so here are some things to keep in mind.

Please note: I am not a lawyer and this is not legal advice. It is based on my experience as a podcaster and author with respect for other creatives. Podcasting is an international medium, and copyright law differs per jurisdiction, so please check your situation carefully. Thanks to Orna Ross at the Alliance of Independent Authors for help with this chapter.

Podcasters need to think about three legal aspects: libel and defamation law, copyright and trademarks, and publicity rights. Bloggers face many of the same questions, and the Electronic Frontier Foundation's Legal Guide to Blogging addresses many issues in more detail.

Copyright

The main thing with copyright law is to be aware of its existence and to question yourself at all times about your use of other people's work. It never hurts to ask a rights-holder or creator for permission. If you're working with an interviewee or creator with a trademark, ensure it is used correctly.

The use of the following is not governed by copyright law, so permission is not required:

- Use of a fact, idea, theory, slogan, title, or short phrase

- Use of works owned by most governments

- Use of creative commons licensed content

- Use of works in the public domain

- Fair use. Any use of a copyrighted work for a limited and "transformative" purpose, such as comment, critique, or parody. This is a grey area, but examples of fair use would be displaying a book cover or work of art while critiquing it, or quoting a few lines from a text while doing a review.

The request to quote from, or otherwise use, the work of another creator should be in writing (email is fine). It should clearly and concisely define the intended use of the work(s), and the assent to the use, also in writing, should be clear and unequivocal.

The Alliance of Independent Authors offers a Copyright Release for an Author Podcast or Video, a licensing agreement which both parties can sign.

Music

Most podcasts use music as part of their intro and outro, and some use sound and other musical elements as part of the show. Music is highly protected, and there are complex ways of tracking it, so you should never use music without the correct licensing and permissions.

Search for **royalty-free music** and go through the available sites. There are lots available with all kinds of music. I used AudioJungle.net for my *Books and Travel Podcast*. I licensed the piece for Mass-Market Reproduction in anticipation of significant downloads over time.

You can also use Creative Commons music, which can be free or donation-based, and many sites will now use the term 'podsafe,' so you know what you can use without a problem.

When I started *The Creative Penn Podcast* back in 2009, I used Creative Commons music created by Kevin MacLeod at Incompetech.com, and even though it was available for free, I donated what I could afford at the time. I still use that music over a decade later because a theme tune becomes part of the show, so choose wisely!

I cite both artists on my podcast home pages, so they are credited for their musical work.

If you know a musician personally and commission music for your podcast, make sure you get written permission for the license to use it.

Artwork

Every podcast requires an image, and again, there are many royalty-free image sites where you can find artwork to use. I have a paid subscription to BigStockPhoto.com as I have several blogs I use images for, and I also use Unsplash.com, which has creative commons images.

Both of my podcasts are businesses, and I use my commissioned logo on top of artwork for my podcast image. If you commission artwork or logos, make sure the copyright is assigned to you or that you have the exclusive license to use the material in your contract with the designer.

Recordings

Copyright law applies when creative works are fixed in a tangible form, for example, when a book is written or when a podcast is recorded.

The copyright to a podcast interview is shared between the people involved. Your words are your copyright, and the interviewee's words are their copyright, but there is also copyright in the recording itself, which will reside with the person who recorded it.

You do not need to register the work for copyright to be applied, although in some jurisdictions, there may be more protection if you do register it. However, a cease and desist letter is often enough for an infringing site to remove content copied from you.

Over the years, my podcast has been downloaded and then re-uploaded to other sites to make revenue for someone else. This is copyright infringement. I reported the infringement, and within a period of weeks, the content was removed. These things may happen, but don't let fear of piracy stop you from creating.

Publicity Rights

Publicity rights govern how an individual's voice, image, or likeness is used in public for commercial purposes. Publicity rights come into play if your podcast brings in any sort of revenue: advertising, sponsorship, branding, patron support, and, arguably, even book sales.

The existence of publicity rights means that if you transmit the voice or image of anyone other than yourself in your podcast or marketing, it is wise to get permission.

The Alliance of Independent Authors advises any podcaster who conducts interviews, whose guests read from their work, perform poetry or drama sequences, sing or produce any kind of spoken or visual content to have guests sign a release form. The Alliance offers a Publicity Release for an Author Podcast or Video, a licensing agreement which both parties can sign.

While this is definitely recommended, I have never used a release form for my show, and in over 600 interviews, I have only been asked to sign such a document a handful of times, and only when the interview was going to be repackaged into a premium course.

There is implied permission in agreeing to go on a podcast, and those involved understand it is for publicity purposes.

I have only had one interviewee back in 2009 ask me to remove an interview after the fact. She was an academic who did not want to be associated with self-publishing back when it was considered 'vanity press.' I should have made my position more clear before we reached the interview stage, and of course, I removed the interview immediately on request.

Things have changed since 2009, and independent creators in every field now garner interest and even respect. Podcasters are taken seriously, and the medium is seen as a good way to boost a profile. If your podcast is a positive experience for all involved, there should be no issues, but if you are concerned, then of course, ask for written permission from your interviewees.

Podcast feed and hosting

Most podcasters think they own their content. After all, they created it.

But if you upload your files to a free hosting service that distributes them across the podcasting world, make sure you know what you have agreed to in the terms of service.

If a service is free, then you are the product.

If a service is free, you may find that you don't own your files once they are uploaded, or the service can insert ads wherever they want for companies you don't agree with.

Read the terms and conditions and email them to yourself with a timestamp, so you know what you agreed to.

There are many free podcasting services, and if you understand what you are agreeing to, and you know your goals for the long term, then go ahead.

Personally, I only use hosting services that I pay for, and I have done this from day one for my website and podcasts. I'm an independent creator, and I like to own and control

my content. I use and recommend both Blubrry and
Libsyn, covered in more detail in chapter 2.12 on podcast
distribution.

* * *

If the concepts in this chapter sound daunting, don't worry.
You just need to know the basics in order to protect your
own work and those of other creators, then you can get
creating!

Questions:

- What do you need to consider around intellectual
  property for your podcast?

- How will you source music for your show?

- How will you find artwork?

- What will you need to consider around interviews
  and working with other people?

2.9 Podcasting equipment and software

I recorded my first podcast episode in March 2009. I lived in Brisbane, Australia, in a Queenslander house — think wooden floors and high ceilings, not the best environment for recording. I phoned my interview subject on a landline and put it on speakerphone, then I held a basic MP3 recorder next to the speaker. You can't get much more basic than that! But the interview went well, and it's still available to listen to at TheCreativePenn.com/episode1

As time went on, I switched to interviews over Skype, I bought a microphone and started using a pop filter and earbuds. It's much better to get started and then improve your equipment over time once you know this is something you want to do rather than investing too much at the start. You'll also need different tools for different situations, so begin with the basics.

Optimize your environment

The worst recording setup will sound a whole lot better if you make sure your environment is quiet and sound-proofed. Go for soft furnishings, carpets and extra sound blankets if you need them. Do a sound test before you start recording, because some sounds can't be heard by the human ear but will get picked up by your device. For example, Wi-Fi signals can make an electronic sound.

Start with the basics

There are plenty of audio apps for mobile devices and tablets and most will come with some kind of sound recorder built in. You can speak directly into the device, or you can buy a Bluetooth or plug-in microphone to make the sound better. Some apps allow you to edit and publish straight to a podcast host, but consider the options in chapter 2.12 on podcast distribution before you commit.

There are also lots of different programs you can use on your laptop or desktop computer. I'm not going to list all the different options because there are so many, with more added all the time, and everyone has different require-ments as well as technical ability, so do some searching for what might be best for you.

My setup has been the same for years. When I record inter-views at my desk, I use a Blue Yeti USB microphone with a pop filter in front of it plugged into my MacBookPro. I use basic iPhone earbuds plugged into the side. I used to use the ATR2100 microphone but switched to BlueYeti after I broke the ATR in a house move. Both are good options.

For video interviews, I have an external HD camera plugged into the Mac and a ring light that sits behind the computer for better lighting.

Interview recording software

If you want to do interviews, there are several options for recording over the internet:

Skype. Still free and perfectly functional after many years. I still use it for my interviews because it gives me the least amount of technical pain, and most people have used it before so I don't have to explain anything. I use Ecamm Recorder with Skype, which is a one-off purchase for video and audio recording. Skype also has a built-in recording option now. You can also use Pamela for the PC or look for other Skype add-ons.

Zoom. There is a free tier, but it has a 40-minute limit on meeting time if you have more than two participants before you have to move to their premium levels.

Zencastr. The free tier has 8 hours of recording per month and records two tracks for better audio quality.

Cleanfeed. There is a free tier, but the professional level has incredibly high-quality recording, so if you want the very best audio, this might be the way to go.

These are the services I have experience with but, of course, there are lots more options. Your choice of recording software should take your guests into account. If you are in a technical niche, then your interviewees will be much more at ease with audio setup, but for many guests, you might need to explain how to use the software.

Always do a short test when you start a new recording session to check the levels on both sides.

If you're recording interviews in person, it's worth considering how often you'll be doing it and how much you can control the environment, because there are all kinds of possibilities for tech.

You can use your mobile device in a quiet environment, and that might be functional enough for your purposes. But you could invest in a digital recorder like the Zoom

H4n, a microphone splitter, and two lavalier (lapel) micro-phones.

Editing software

Once you have your raw audio, the next step is editing. You can work with a freelancer, covered in chapter 2.14, but you will need a budget for that, and most podcasters do everything themselves when starting out. To be honest, it is not that complicated to do basic audio editing, and there are plenty of free tutorials online as well as free software, so set aside a few hours and give it a try.

If you're putting together a highly produced show with multiple audio clips, music and sound effects, you will need a more comprehensive editing system than someone who adds an intro and outro onto an interview recording. Your choice will also depend on how much you want to learn about audio editing. Personally, I have kept it pretty simple over the years! Here are some software options:

Audacity. For Mac and Windows. This free software is fantastic if you only want the basics. I used it for years.

Amadeus Pro. Mac only. I switched to Amadeus Pro because it is more intuitive for the Mac user, but I still only use the basics.

Screenflow. Mac only. You can do video editing with Screenflow, so if you're producing a video podcast, you can use this for both video and audio exports. Camtasia is the equivalent for the PC.

If you want to get serious about audio editing, check out **Adobe Audition** or **Avid Pro Tools**. These programs contain far more functionality than the average podcaster will need, but if you want to learn sound production for podcasting and audiobooks, it might be worth doing some tutorials.

It doesn't have to be perfect

Podcasts are (mostly) free and listeners will forgive a lot if they get value from your show. If you don't have the best microphone, start anyway. If your environment is not completely silent, start anyway. Focus on serving your audience and improve your tools along the way.

Questions:

- What equipment and software do you need right now in order to get started?

- What might you consider investing in later?

- What skills do you need to practice?

2.10 Podcast structure

Podcasting is not just about turning on a microphone, talking for a bit, and then clicking Publish. You can do that, but it's unlikely to be successful.

Your podcast should have a consistent structure. As people tune in, they get to know what to listen out for and what to skip over. Of course, this will change over time, but it's good to understand what you might need in advance.

Here's my structure for *The Creative Penn Podcast*. Yours won't be exactly the same, but as you listen to other shows, note the different segments and how you might incorporate aspects into your own production.

Intro

This is a pre-recorded introduction to the show played over the theme tune every week. Intellectual property considerations for music are covered in chapter 2.8. Consistency in repetition means that listeners instantly associate you with this music and even get to know the words by heart over time. Make sure you identify yourself by name and what your podcast is about, as some new people will join the show each time.

Welcome

This is an introductory statement that welcomes listeners back to your show. I use something like the following each week:

> Hello Creatives, I'm Joanna Penn. This is episode number 490 of the podcast and it's 2 February 2020 as I record this.

This welcome serves several purposes. I use the term 'Creatives' so my listeners feel part of the community, and if they don't identify as creatives, they will probably turn off at this point. Creatives as a term resonates with my business, The Creative Penn, and for *Books and Travel*, I say, 'Hello, travelers.' You don't have to do this, but if you do, use a word that denotes your community.

I note the episode number as social proof and also to indicate that there is a backlist of episodes for people to download if they want to. I include the date for *The Creative Penn Podcast* because some of my material is time-sensitive. I will also explain what's coming up in today's interview, so listeners know if they want to stick around for that.

Regular host segments

Many of my audience for *The Creative Penn Podcast* tune in for the introduction and updates and don't listen to the interview unless it's relevant to their situation.

I have several different segments that I include at different times. I rarely use all of them in every episode, but always do one or two.

My segments include:

Publishing and book marketing news

This is any industry news that will impact my audience. Including news is both a blessing and a curse for the podcast. It's good because some people listen in every week just for this segment even if they don't want the interview, but it's bad because it dates the show, and the content is not evergreen.

Futurist segment

While the publishing news section is about the current state, I also love to share what's happening in the world of artificial intelligence (AI) and future technologies that will impact authors and publishing over the next five to ten years. This is a topic I read about all the time, so I enjoy sharing this information. I know that some listeners skip over it, and others tune in especially for this section. You can't please everyone all the time, so focus on what you find interesting.

Personal update

I'm a writer first, and my credibility is based on continuing to write, publish, and make a living from my writing. I share my writing update as social proof, but also as marketing as I talk about my work in progress, and also as relationship building with my community. If I'm going through a hard time as an author, I talk about it, because my listeners go through the same things.

I didn't do a personal update for the first few years of my show because I thought no one would care. Then one day, a listener emailed and said they wanted to know more. I am forever grateful for that nudge!

Your regular host segments will be different, but they are important because your audience cares about you. Don't make it all about your guests, because they are only on for a short time. You are the constant. Be sure to share your life and what interests you, and in that way, you will build a relationship with your listeners over time.

Useful stuff

In this segment, I talk about webinars, books, or other podcast episodes that might be useful to the listeners. This is often time-sensitive.

Community segment

Podcasting is not just a one-way broadcast. Your listeners will post comments on your show notes and social media, as well as emailing thoughts and writing reviews and articles. This might not happen immediately, but it will happen if you keep producing over time.

I read selected comments and tweets from my community and answer appropriate questions if they come up. This gives the sense that people are heard, and listeners are often thrilled when they hear their name on the show.

Advertising and Patreon

At some point, you might consider monetizing your podcast, covered in detail in chapter 2.19, so it's good to get your listeners into the habit of listening to some kind of promotion. You could start by mentioning your books, products and services, for example, "Today's podcast is sponsored by my book …" and then give the title, description, and a call to action.

In this segment, I do an ad read for my primary corporate sponsor or play an audio clip from them. I'll also thank my new patrons on Patreon and give a call to action to support the show if they find it useful.

Interview or main show content

This will be the longest segment, featuring the interview or your own material if you record alone. Sometimes I will create a solo episode on a topic and pre-record it, before adding the introduction just before the show goes out.

Host round-up and what's coming next week

I've only started doing this in the last few years, but many in the audience have said they like it. I do a little round-up of the interview and make any final comments before revealing next week's guest and topic, so the listeners know what's coming. This is very short, often less than a minute.

Outro

This is your pre-recorded outro over your theme music. Thank your listeners, and make sure you include a call to action. This might be to sign up for your email list and get something of value, or to leave a review.

Questions:

- What are the different segments that you enjoy on your favorite podcasts? What might be effective for your audience?

- What material will be evergreen, and what will be newsworthy about your show? What will keep people coming back?

- Have you scripted and recorded your intro and outro?

2.11 How to be a great podcast host

"What most listeners and aspiring podcasters miss is that there is a big difference between being spontaneous and sounding spontaneous. There are often hours of prep work that go into a podcast episode, done by the host and/or producer before the microphones are turned on."

Eric Nuzum, Make Noise: A Creator's Guide to Podcasting and Great Audio Storytelling

I've been on hundreds of podcast and radio interviews over the last decade as well as interviewing over 500 guests on my own shows. If you're going to have an interview-based podcast, you need to be a great host. Here are my tips for making your show a good experience for all involved.

Research your potential guests

Once your show becomes established, you will get pitched all the time, but at the beginning, you will need to research and pitch guests yourself.

Don't start by asking the most famous person in your niche. You need to practice, and they will also need social proof before they spend precious time on your show. As a ballpark, once you make it past 50 episodes, then you are more likely to be able to pitch bigger-name guests. If they say no, don't worry, you can always ask again a year later when you have more credibility in the niche.

When you pitch them for your show:

- State **why you want them to come on** and include something personal that demonstrates you know what they do and understand their value

- **Include what you want to talk about**, which could be a headline or a couple of related topics

- **Address why this might interest them,** for example, it's a tangential niche they might not usually reach

- **Be sure to specify the podcast name**, number of episodes, reach in terms of number of downloads plus any email subscriber numbers or social media followers, as well as a website link so they can check out your professional site

When I get a pitch email, the first thing I do is check out the website and listen to a few minutes of a show to see if it's a good fit.

Once you've booked a guest, listen to other interviews with them. Understand what they want to talk about and what would benefit them the most as well as helping your audience.

Prepare for the interview

Podcast interviews should be a positive experience for all involved, especially as one of the best outcomes is a private conversation with an influencer in your niche. You want the guest to think that you are professional and courteous and to recommend you to others, as well as sharing the interview with their audience, which they won't do if they have a bad time.

Some of my worst experiences as an interviewee have included:

- The host who started recording as soon as we got on the line and would not edit what should have been an initial few minutes of getting to know each other. This put me on the back foot and annoyed me for the rest of the interview. I felt like his aim had been to catch me out, and I did not share that interview publicly although it is still out there.

- The host who asked me questions that didn't relate to my experience and made incorrect assumptions about my expertise. This made both of us sound bad and could have been prevented by even a few minutes of research.

- The host who spent most of the show doing a monologue and occasionally bringing me in and then carrying on with their own agenda. It was a waste of my time. If you're going to do an interview, make it a conversation. You can do your additional chat before or after the segment.

You can prevent these kinds of experiences as a host by preparing beforehand and sending questions over to the guest, so they feel some confidence that you know what you're doing. Some people prefer not to know questions in advance, but in my experience, the majority of guests want to see the direction of the interview beforehand.

I definitely want questions in advance when I am a guest. I get quite nervous with hosts that just say, "Don't worry, it's a natural conversation." Too often, those turn out to be poorly prepared and not very useful to the audience or for me as a guest.

Practicalities of the interview

You will often be booking interviews in different **time zones.** Use Calendly.com or another calendar app that enables the guest to choose a slot and also change it as necessary. This also gives a space to ask questions. I ask for a Skype name and a basic bio, which gives me a start to prepare the interview. Don't go overboard with this though. I have seen some pre-show booking forms with lots of questions and this can be a turn-off for the guest.

Send a confirmation email a few days before with up-to-date technical information, questions, or at least a direction or topic for the podcast. You could also let the guest know the audience for your podcast, so they know what angle to address. For example, I do a lot of interviews about 'how to write a book,' but it's a very different topic if I'm addressing an indie fiction podcast vs. a show for speakers who want to use a non-fiction book as a business card.

Make sure you have tested your technical settings, downloaded the latest version of software, shut down, and rebooted your system. This may sound like overkill, but if you haven't logged in for even a few days, your recording software might need updating. Once you update, you should always shut down and restart. This also makes sure you have closed down other applications, so your system runs at its best. Technical issues are inevitable once in a while, but do your best to avoid them.

Be on time. Call the guest as soon as the clock ticks over to the allotted time. If anyone is late, it should be them and if they are late, be understanding and friendly. Do not go over the allotted time slot, even if things go wrong. It's better to cut the interview short than to go over time.

Greet the guest and spend a minute or two setting them at ease and also **check their technical settings.** You need to get into the interview without too much chat, but you also need to ensure the recording will work. I usually ask about their day and often ask they adjust certain things, for example, use a headset or a different device. Make it easy and pleasant for the guest as much as you can.

Tell the guest when you are about to start recording, so they are ready and know when they are 'on the record.'

Make it a conversation. Have your questions ready and notes by your side or on the screen, but don't read them. Use your notes to guide the conversation but also write down interesting things to follow up on as you talk. Change the order of questions based on what comes up or follow your curiosity and ask new things. Most guests are fine with this as long as you're not trying to catch them out. Ask the questions your audience want to know. Anything that comes up in your mind is likely to be something they are thinking about, too.

I write down notes using the guest's language, so I can circle back to previous topics using their words. This helps make the interview a coherent whole rather than a straight Q&A.

Be flexible and be prepared to change tack. Don't keep doggedly running down your list of questions. If something has been answered already, don't ask it again.

Make the guest sound good. Don't try to catch them out. Think about throwing a ball and wanting them to catch it, then throw it back. It's a fun game, not an aggressive pursuit — unless, of course, you have a podcast in a niche where that is the goal.

If things do go wrong on a technical or personal level, just be a human being about it. **Patience, humor, and understanding go a long way.** People are people, and most guests will understand a setback. Just make sure you try to avoid the same issue again if it's your fault.

Thank the guest at the end of the interview and give them a chance to promote whatever they want to promote. End the conversation and tell the guest that the recording has stopped. You might have a few minutes of personal chat at the end, or they might have to leave for another appointment.

After the interview

Email to thank the guest for their time and send them links for the episode when it goes out. Don't expect them to remember it's going live later or to listen to it.

Do not expect the guest to promote the show and certainly don't demand it. If they enjoyed the experience and it's useful to their audience, they will promote it. If you share it on social media, tag them, and they might re-share it.

If the guest also has a podcast, do not expect to be invited back. If your expertise is useful for their audience, they might invite you, but it is never a quid pro quo.

"No amount of research or question-writing
or prep will ever serve you better than just following
your own instincts … What defines a good interviewer
truly is someone who is comfortable using themselves
as a proxy for the audience."

*Eric Nuzum, Make Noise: A Creator's Guide to
Podcasting and Great Audio Storytelling*

Questions:

- Make a list of 10 people you'd like to interview. Do your research on them and craft a pitch asking them to come on your show.

- How will you prepare for the interview in order to make it a good experience for your guest?

- How will you make sure the conversation goes smoothly and is useful for your audience as well as pleasant for your guest?

- How will you handle it if things go wrong?

2.12 Podcast distribution

Once you have a finished audio file ready to go out into the world, you need a distribution service so your show will appear in all the directories and podcast apps. You don't need to submit to each one manually. Just use an established platform, and they will distribute your content everywhere.

There are many options to choose from and more starting up all the time, so here are some considerations to think about.

If a service is free, then you are the product

If a podcast hosting and distribution service is free, look at the terms and conditions for what they ask in return. All businesses have a revenue model, and they will have to make money from that service at some point. If you are not paying them directly, they will monetize your content in other ways.

For many free podcast hosts, it's advertising. If you use a service for free, they can put ads into your show. You may have no control over what companies can advertise, and you may or may not receive a share of that revenue. It might also be data, where the service collects and owns information based on listeners' behavior.

If you're an independent creator intent on building your own brand and making podcasting part of your business, pay for hosting in the same way as you would pay to host your website. Only then can you be sure that you both own and control your content, branding, and revenue model.

Podcast hosting services

If you decide to use a premium host, consider what features appeal to you, and compare pricing and benefits. What is important to you as a podcaster?

It's also worth considering longevity in the market and the business model of the company you're considering. Since podcasting took off in 2014, a number of new companies have emerged, many of which have burned through initial funding and disappeared or been bought.

Two of the longest-running companies are Libsyn and Blubrry, both of which offer scalable hosting packages, distribution to all the podcast apps and players, and various levels of reporting. They are also IAB certified, which means that their statistics can be trusted for measuring downloads, whereas sometimes downloads are inflated for advertising revenue purposes. Advertisers may look for this certification in future to ensure their money is invested in the best way.

There are plenty of other hosting companies, and the space can seem confusing and crowded. Opportunities also change over time. It's worth searching online for the best podcast hosting services. Limit your search to the last six months, then search for comparisons between each service and Libsyn and Blubrry.

My hosting and distribution choice

I started podcasting in 2009, and there were only a few choices back then, although it's good to know that the company I chose is still around and one of the most respected. I also decided to be independent, so it was important to retain as much control as possible.

I use Blubrry to host and distribute my files, although I did use Amazon S3 hosting before it became too expensive. I have always used the Blubrry PowerPress plugin for Word-Press to distribute my feed to the various players, and I also use Blubrry IAB Certified Professional Podcast Statistics to get download numbers for my advertising partners.

I'm very happy with Blubrry and find it simple to use with good reporting and help if you need it.

> As I use Blubrry as my primary host, I'm an affiliate of their service. You can use my link at:
>
> TheCreativePenn.com/podcasthost
>
> or just go to Blubrry.com

YouTube for audio podcasting

If you do a video podcast or vlog, then YouTube is the obvious choice for distribution, but many people also use YouTube for audio-only, so don't discount it.

I did my podcast interviews as videos on YouTube for over ten years, but I switched to putting the full audio episode on YouTube in early 2019. I fully expected my channel to die, but surprisingly, my subscribers grew even faster, and I still do occasional video episodes to supplement the content.

You can check it out at:

YouTube.com/thecreativepenn

How much does podcast hosting cost?

Most podcast hosting services have scalable plans. They have a starter plan, usually around $5-$40 a month, which increases based on storage and/or downloads.

If you have a massively popular podcast, you can expect to pay a few hundred dollars per month, but this may take years to get to, so you have time to monetize your show.

Need more technical help?

I can't help with technical questions about setup, podcast hosting, and distribution, but there are lots of people who can assist.

Each podcast hosting service has a customer team ready to help, and there are also podcasts and blogs about podcasting where the hosts have far more knowledge than I do. Search and see what resonates with you.

> I personally know and recommend Colin Gray, The Podcast Host. You can listen to his show, *PodCraft*, if you want to get a taste of his work. He has courses and lots more help at his Podcast Academy:
>
> TheCreativePenn.com/podcastacademy

Questions:

- What do you need to consider around distribution for your podcast? What are the pros and cons of paying for hosting?

- Have you researched the different services available? What would work best for your situation?

2.13 Show notes and transcripts

Your primary output as a podcaster is an audio file that listeners download to their device, but most podcasters also provide useful show notes, and many create transcripts of interviews.

These accompanying notes can range from basic bullet points to thousands of words and images to support the audio material. Here's why show notes and transcripts are important.

Links to supporting material, as well as advertising and marketing

Audio is a terrible medium for links, but the nature of the internet, especially for newsworthy content, is about linking to sources. If I read a headline from *Wired* magazine, I can quote the source, but the link to the original article has to go in the show notes, as I can't read the URL out loud.

If I'm interviewing someone and they mention a particular topic, but we don't have time to go into it, I can link to it in the show notes.

If you have corporate advertisers, you will link to them in the show notes, and many provide a special link to measure click-throughs, even though the number of downloads is the primary measure.

If you want to sell your own books, services, and products, or include affiliate offers, then you also want to list links on a show notes page.

It's worth spending the extra time making sure your supporting material is professional and useful, especially if you intend to monetize your show.

Search Engine Optimization

Google Podcasts and Apple Podcasts only started indexing audio episodes in mid-2019. Before this, indexing only happened through the show notes and transcript page, so they were critical for your show to be found on the internet.

But even now, those pages are still useful because podcast indexing still works from transcription generated by the various services. There are inherent issues with AI transcription, especially if you have a non-US-English accent or you are in a niche that has particularly difficult words, for example, medical terms or place names. If you have a transcript and/or show notes, the podcast services are likely to use that to enhance their own indexing, so it's well worth producing them.

Accessibility

Notes and transcripts are great for making sure that people who can't hear can still access your information.

Some people don't want to listen to your show but may still read your notes and transcript. I've had a surprising number of people tell me that they only ever read the podcast and never listen.

Creating show notes and transcripts

Your process for the creation of episode show notes will depend on the kind of content you produce and your budget.

If I'm recording a solo show, I prepare the accompanying article beforehand, complete with links and notes. I then record the episode.

For an interview show, the transcript is produced from the audio recording, and then the show notes are done afterward.

Options for transcription include:

- **AI-created transcription.** I use Descript.com as it also allows me to excerpt snippets of audio. You can also use Otter.ai or other services for AI transcription. It may not be perfect, but it is often free.

- **Human transcription.** This will be more exact, but it will usually cost around US$1 for one minute of audio. Services include speechpad.com and rev.com, both of which I have used personally and can recommend.

You will have to clean up the transcript and any notes, format the associated blog post, and add any shareable images.

Some companies specialize in end-to-end podcast production, but you will need a budget. You can also work with freelancers to take care of different aspects, as I do.

Images

Since podcasting is an audio medium, you might not think you need images. However, if you consider the show notes or associated article as something to be consumed separately, you can still use images to bring it alive. If you want the episode to be shared on social media, it's also a good idea to use images within your show notes.

I use a lot of images on my podcast episodes and articles on BooksAndTravel.page because visual media enriches a travel conversation.

There are various apps and plugins for your website that you can use for social sharing. I use Social Warfare Plugin for WordPress, and I create shareable images using Canva. com. I use my own photos, license them from BigStock-Photo, or use a creative commons site like Unsplash. com. Make sure you use royalty-free images and check permissions to avoid any copyright issues, as covered in chapter 2.8.

Questions:

- Why are show notes and transcripts useful for you and also for your audience?

- How will you generate your show notes and/or transcript?

- What kinds of images will you include in your show notes?

2.14 Collaboration and freelancers

You don't have to podcast alone, and in fact, the most successful and long-running podcasters all work with a team. You might have a co-host to share the load of creation and marketing or even multiple co-hosts like the long-running *Writing Excuses Podcast*. But if you create your podcast alone or interview guests, as I do, you can still work with a team of freelancers to help with editing, distribution, and marketing.

Should you co-host a podcast?

"Co-hosting a podcast lessens performance anxiety because you have another person to help carry the load. Whether it's pre-production or post-production, the work can be distributed, which makes it easier to sustain the effort over months or years.

The only downside to co-hosting is that you must be in alignment with your partner. Compromise is crucial, and it's important to understand that in any partnership, you won't always get your own way."

J. Thorn, co-host of four podcasts over the last decade as well as host of his own show at TheAuthorLife.com

There are both pros and cons with co-hosting a podcast. On the plus side, you get to split the work and share the load, as well as create something new with (presumably) someone you enjoy working with.

But you have to consider what happens when things get complicated — for example, one of you wants to stop doing the show; one of you feels like the other isn't doing enough work; or there are hosting costs, and one person feels they are paying too much.

If you spend months or years building a podcast with someone, putting time, energy, and most likely, money into the project and then things get difficult; you need to know what will happen next. What will you do about the website, the podcast feed, the content created, perhaps even the money generated, and things like the email list or the branding.

I am naturally a long-term thinker, and when I start a project, it usually has a business plan around it that will take several years to execute. I have never co-hosted a podcast because most shows don't last long. You need to decide what's right for you, but if you do decide to co-host, then make sure all parties understand their responsibilities upfront and discuss possibilities for future success and failure.

Rachael Herron, author and podcaster at RachaelHerron. com says,

> "I love co-hosting! I've done *The Writer's Well* podcast with J. Thorn now for almost three years. I'm in the luxurious and privileged position of having zero cons of doing it, and the pros of it go on and on. I show up and talk to one of my best friends about topics I really care about (living a writer's healthy life, mentally and physically).
>
> It's a short show, just 25 minutes on average, so it doesn't take much time out from my writing.

J sends the files to his assistant to post, so even on his end, there's very little work for this particular show (of his many). We don't have sponsors or even do intros or outros. We show up and say hello. We chat, and then we share. We have an amazingly supportive listenership who leave us the most thoughtful comments, and some of them even support our Patreon.

I have my own solo show, *How Do You Write*, on which I interview successful writers about their writing processes, and while I love doing it, it weighs much heavier on me than the show with J. *The Writer's Well* is simply a joy in every single way."

Freelancers and work for hire

The rise in podcasting has also led to a raft of new companies that work with podcasters. You can get a full-service team who will turn your raw audio into a finished product complete with show notes and marketing images — but it will cost you at least several hundred dollars per episode. Chapter 2.19 goes into how you could make the money to pay for this kind of service, but most podcasters start out doing everything themselves and outsource pieces over time.

You can also hire freelancers to work per hour or per episode, which is likely to work out cheaper. I work with Dan, a freelance sound engineer for my shows. I add my files to Dropbox, and he puts the shows together as finished audio. My virtual assistant, Alexandra, does the show notes and transcription editing, as detailed in chapter 2.15 on workflow.

You can also find voice talent as work for hire. Whether you need a voiceover for your podcast intro, or a full character voice actor for your podcast fiction, you can hire freelancers for the role.

Ask for recommendations of freelancers within your network or ask your community if you have a podcast already (which is how I found Alexandra and Dan). You can also look at sites like Upwork.com, PeoplePerHour.com or Fiverr.com to find audio production specialists. Make sure you have a contract that assigns copyright for the sound production and ensure you have the right permissions as covered in chapter 2.8 on intellectual property.

When working with freelancers, use Google Sheets or another shared document to plan and track the progress of episodes through to production.

Podcast collectives

While co-hosting relates to a particular show, a podcast collective is usually a group of podcasts under a specific brand on a common theme. This brings the benefit of group negotiation for advertising, cross-marketing, and community.

If you are considering a collective, make sure you understand what is required of members, as well as what control you might give up in exchange for the benefits. You might also want to check how a podcast can leave the collective if things change in the future.

"In October 2019, the *Big Gay Fiction Podcast* became one of the shows making up the Frolic Podcast Network. One of the hopes is that combining multiple podcasts can make it more attractive to sponsors. Beyond any possible financial gain is also the power of cross-promotion so that listeners of other shows hear about us — if you're already listening to a show about romance, it's possible you're interested in checking out others.

Among authors, we see networks formed all the time — authors who write similar things band together for promotions, discuss trends, possibly create universes, and write books together. The same is true with podcasting."

Jeff Adams and Will Knauss, authors and hosts of the Big Gay Fiction Podcast and the Big Gay Author Podcast.

Questions:

- What are the pros and cons of co-hosting a podcast?

- If you are considering co-hosting, write down what you would bring to the arrangement and what skills you would need in a co-host. How will you make this work for the long term?

- How could you use freelancers to make podcasting easier? What tasks could you outsource?

- If you're interested in a podcast collective, what are the benefits and the things to watch out for?

2.15 Podcast workflow and tools

There are lots of moving parts to a podcast, so in this chapter, I share my workflow and specific tools so you can see the sequence and timings of everything that needs to be done. It might sound daunting, but remember, podcasting is one of the pillars of my full-time creative business, so my process is quite extensive.

However, it can be simple, as author and podcaster Barry Pearman noted about his *Turning the Page Podcast* on empowering your mental health.

"One of the blocks I had about podcasting was that a podcast has to be interview style and 30-60 minutes long. In other words, it's a huge commitment for someone who has a full-time job and writing is the sideline. So I decided to make it super simple and not allow it to impact my first love of writing.

I simply read my latest blog post, record it on Audacity, load it to Podbean, which distributes to the other platforms. It took a bit of time to set up, but now it takes about 30 minutes a week for me to be a podcaster. The show is around 10-12 minutes, some intro and outro music by a friend of mine, and it's done. Simple."

Every podcaster has a slightly different process and prefers different tools, so you don't need to replicate mine exactly. My process has also been modified over a decade. At the beginning, I did everything myself. Now, I have a team of freelancers, and there are many more tools available.

At least a month before the scheduled podcast live date

- Decide on a guest and research their background. Pitch guest and book time for an interview with Calendly.com [Joanna - 30 minutes]

1 week before the interview date

- Prepare questions and send them to the guest along with confirmation of the interview and technical details. [Joanna - 30 minutes]

Interview day

- Conduct and record the interview over Skype with eCamm Recorder. Save the interview audio file to Dropbox on the shared drive and add the MP3 to Descript or Speechpad for the transcript. [Joanna - 60 minutes]

At least 1 week before the podcast live date

- Edit transcription and create a blog post with the transcript and show notes [Alexandra - 60-120 minutes. The time taken for this step depends on the length of the interview, and any difficult accents or research for spelling. These are common on the *Books and Travel Podcast* as it has an international focus.]

3 days before the podcast live date

- Prepare and record the regular segments for the podcast episode with Amadeus Pro. Save to Dropbox. [Joanna - 60 minutes]

- Write the introduction for the blog post with any links, notes, and sponsorship details as well as doing a final edit of the transcription. Prepare podcast images on Canva.com [Joanna - 30 minutes]

- Edit the interview audio file together with the intro music, weekly segments, end matter, and outro. [Dan - 60 minutes]

- Upload the audio file to Auphonic.com for meta-data and leveling. Upload the finished audio file to Blubrry hosting service and update the blog post with the details. [Dan - 20 minutes]

1 day before the podcast live date

- Review, check and schedule the podcast episode. [Joanna - 10 minutes]

- Download the audio and use it to make a video in Screenflow. Upload the video to YouTube with show notes. [Joanna - 20 minutes]

On the podcast live date

- Add the episode to TheCreativePenn.com/podcast and add a link and a message on Patreon if it's a sponsored show. Share and schedule on social media with Buffer. Email and thank the guest with links to the episode. [Joanna - 20 minutes]

After the podcast live date

- Excerpt audio snippets from the episode with Descript. [Joanna - 20 minutes]

- Turn the audio snippet into an audiogram for social media on Headliner app. [Sacha - 20 minutes] This is a recent addition to the workflow and is usually done in batches, rather than per episode.

- Schedule further social media sharing on Buffer [Alexandra or Joanna - 20 minutes]

Total time:

- 300 minutes, or around 5 hours per show [Joanna]

- 80-120 minutes [Alexandra]

- 80 minutes [Dan]

- 20 minutes [Sacha]

This workflow should give you a good idea of the various tasks involved, as well as the time it can take to produce a finished podcast of around one hour. The total time is around 8 hours per episode. Bear in mind that a highly scripted and produced show will take much longer.

If I'm doing a solo episode, I might spend many more hours on writing, researching, and preparing the material. You can understand why I consider the podcast an important part of my creative body of work as well as a critical part of my business!

This workload is why so many podcasters give up. It's a lot of effort, so you have to have a good reason to keep going for the long term.

Questions:

- What might your podcast workflow look like?

- How can you make the time to achieve this on a regular basis or how can you budget for freelance help?

2.16 How to launch a podcast

Launching a podcast is a bit like launching a book as an independent author. You have grand dreams of many thousands of people turning up to listen or read or buy, but in reality, it takes time for anything to build.

So the bad news is, even if you launch with a well-organized fanfare, very few people will know your podcast exists on day one.

But it's also good news because it means you can practice and make mistakes and sort out your technical issues before lots of people hear about you. You can grow in capability and professionalism so that when things do start to take off — which they will if you're in a reasonably popular niche and you are consistent over the long term — your new listeners will subscribe and stick around.

I did a mini-launch for *Books and Travel*, but with *The Creative Penn Podcast*, I just started putting episodes out one day, and it grew from there. If you want to launch your show, here are some ideas.

(1) Plan your launch content

Podcast listeners behave in the same way that readers do. If they find a content producer they like and resonate with — an author or a podcaster — then they want more than one episode or one book. If you have multiple episodes available, the new listener may download them all and subscribe, which is exactly what you want. If you only have one episode, that might not be enough to get them to subscribe.

I launched with five episodes on *Books and Travel*, including two solo shows, which took a lot longer to produce than the interviews. Many professional podcasters suggest starting with at least ten episodes, as it boosts your initial download numbers.

I planned the content several months in advance because I knew I wanted to interview specific people and write about my own travels. I have my content schedule in Google Sheets, which I share with my virtual assistant and sound producer, so we know the dates for each episode.

Try to be strategic around who you interview for the launch content. For example, other podcasters might share your new show with their listeners. It's worth planning these pitches well in advance so you can develop relationships before pitching.

(2) Choose a day to officially announce your new show

If you have an audience already, you can announce it to them. If you're just starting out, then write it somewhere visible and keep to that deadline. I told my audience at *The Creative Penn Podcast* that I would launch my new show during my tenth-anniversary edition in March 2019. That gave me a date to aim for, and you *do* need a date, or you will procrastinate forever. The To Do list never stops, and you will never be completely ready, so set your date and stick to it.

Importantly, make sure you have your technical setup ready at least a few days prior, so you have time to work out the glitches. You don't want to announce a new show, only to find your feed hasn't been approved by Apple, and the show isn't in the podcast apps, so make sure it is available before you announce it.

(3) Plan your marketing

One of the best ways to advertise a new show is to go on other podcasts. Most shows batch content and record early, so pitch shows that might work for you well in advance. You can talk about your book topic or niche experience, and make sure to mention your podcast in the call to action at the end of the show. If people like your voice and what you have to say, some of them will try your podcast and (hopefully) subscribe.

(4) Create content for the launch — and the weeks after

You will need to have an intense period of content preparation in order to have several episodes available on launch and more ready to go out in the weeks following that initial phase.

Make sure you have time to prepare material, conduct interviews, up-skill on any technology you need, create accompanying notes, and make your show as professional as possible. Believe me, it takes longer than you think!

(5) Optimize your website

As part of your podcast call to action, you will direct listeners to your website to sign up for your email list, or perhaps check out your books, or some other action that will lead (eventually) to revenue. Money is only one aspect of success, but it's good to design for it early in the process.

Make sure your website is professional and optimized for mobile browsing as well as email signups. Ensure your About page is up to date, and any book pages have links to the various book stores.

If you need help with your website or email list, check out my tutorials at:

TheCreativePenn.com/authorwebsite

(6) Create marketing material

Prepare your marketing material in advance, for example, audio snippets of the interview with accompanying shareable images optimized for the various social media platforms. You might also want to set aside some budget for Facebook Ads or other paid advertising to your niche market.

If your show is newsworthy or local, then it might be worth pitching a press release to related media. Remember that the podcast itself is not the story, and neither is your book, but there might be an angle for your niche that works. More marketing ideas in chapter 2.17.

(7) Aiming for New and Noteworthy?

The Apple iTunes Podcast New and Noteworthy listing is a bit like an author trying to hit a bestseller list in the first week of launch. You can do lots of things to try and make it happen, but it's ultimately out of your control.

However, there are a few things you can do to maximize your chances of hitting the listing in your first week if that's important for you.

Make sure your podcast metadata is completed and include multiple categories as well as a description, your show name and image. Check for underserved categories as well as looking at the stores in different countries, as you could hit a list somewhere other than the over-competitive US market.

Launch with a number of episodes and publish frequently during the first eight weeks, so you get lots of downloads, and make sure you focus on getting reviews in that initial period. Things change all the time, so search online for the most up-to-date tips on hitting the list.

If this matters to you, by all means, go for it! But personally, I don't check the charts. I have never hit any podcast list that I know of, but *The Creative Penn Podcast* is in the top 5% of all podcasts downloaded according to stats presented at Podcast Movement 2019, and I make the equivalent of a full-time income from the show. Delivering a consistent quality experience over time is far more important than an initial spike or list screenshot, and the same applies to your author business.

Serve your audience, build for the long term, and you will achieve success.

Questions:

- What do you need to prepare in advance of your launch date?

- Have you decided on your launch date? Will you have time to get everything done by then?

- Do you have a content and production schedule, so you know when everything needs to be done? Does this also stretch into the weeks after launch, when you will need to post regular content to gain traction?

- Is your website optimized for possible traffic and email signups?

- Have you created your marketing material?

- How will you measure a successful launch?

2.17 How to market a podcast

Now your podcast is out in the world, you need to make sure that you attract new listeners as well as retaining the old. I much prefer this kind of consistent marketing over time, as I've found that many podcasts launch well, but few deliver value for the long term. Word of mouth kicks in if you keep creating a quality experience on a regular basis, as well as a growth in reputation, so listenership expands naturally. Here are some other things you can do to market your show.

(1) Create a podcast home page on your website

Most long-term, successful podcasters have a website with a lot more than just a podcast. My site, TheCreativePenn. com has articles, books, courses, tutorials, and tools, as well as my show, so it's important to have a home page with all the links to your show over time as well as subscription buttons for the most popular podcast apps.

I list my episodes in reverse order and link through to the show notes, as well as feature links to the podcast apps, sponsor logos, review quotes, my Patreon link, and credit for the music and freelancers who work on my show.

You can find my podcast home pages at:

TheCreativePenn.com/podcast

and BooksAndTravel.page/listen

(2) Submit to every podcast directory

Make sure your show is available everywhere. Your podcast distributor will submit your feed to the main ones, but you might need to add your feed manually on other directories and sites, for example, Tune In for Amazon Alexa, or Spotify. You only have to do this once, and then new episodes will automatically appear.

(3) Use Search Engine Optimized (SEO) headlines for your episodes

Think about how a potential listener might find your show. They are not likely to know your guest by name or care what number episode it is, but they might click and listen if the topic interests them. Compare these two examples:

- Episode 448: Lisa M Lilly

- Happiness, Anxiety and Writing with a Full-Time Day Job with Lisa M Lilly [Episode 448]

I see way too many shows with just the episode number and name of the guest, but it's far more important to start with the main topic of the show so that listeners can decide whether it's worth their time.

As a listener, I use the search function within the Apple Podcast app on my phone to find new shows to listen to. I'll type in a topic or sometimes a guest name if I want to listen to a particular author and then download a whole load of episodes. I might end up subscribing to some of those shows if they resonate, but the key to finding them is through well-optimized headlines.

(4) Create shareable social media images and audiograms

Use Canva.com to create images with your show art and quotes that will resonate with your audience on the various social platforms. Use a scheduling service like Bufferapp so you can batch the creation and publishing process.

Use Headliner.app or Wavve.com to create playable audiograms that you can schedule and use in social media to promote your show. An audiogram is a snippet of audio that plays as a video of a waveform over an image. You can create them in different sizes, for example, Instagram Stories or Twitter, or create videos to use on YouTube.

You can play an audiogram from the *Books and Travel Podcast* on Twitter at:

TheCreativePenn.com/podcastaudiogram

(5) Make your show notes shareable

Use social media sharing buttons on your website so the audio file, as well as quotes and images, can be shared directly. I use the Social Warfare plugin for WordPress to create 'Click to Tweet' quotes as well as images sized specifically for Facebook and Pinterest.

(6) Add a link in your email signature for your show

This is an easy one. Just go into your email settings and update your signature. Add your podcast name and tagline plus a link to the show home page or the most popular podcast app links in your niche.

(7) Email your list when a new episode comes out

If your podcast is part of your wider online business eco-system, you need to build an email list.

> If you haven't done this already, you can find tips in my tutorial at TheCreativePenn.com/setup-email-list

Once you have an email list, you need to stay in touch with people regularly, and sending new episodes of your podcast is a great way to provide new content. I email my Creative Penn audience every few weeks and include links to my top episodes, and I have a monthly reading list on *Books and Travel* that includes the podcast links.

(8) Give your interview guests everything they need to share their appearance easily

If your guests feel like their interview would be useful to their followers, they may share it with their network. When the show is live, email them to say thank you and send a link to the page and any shareable images they might find useful.

(9) Pitch for interviews on other podcasts

This is one of the most effective ways to grow your audience because podcast listeners usually listen to several shows in a niche. If they hear you on a show they like and enjoy what you have to say, they are only a few clicks away from subscribing to your show. Make sure you include a call to action that mentions your podcast (and/or audiobooks) at the end of the interview.

Once you become more established, people will invite you on their show, but don't be afraid to get started by pitching both inside and outside of your niche. More about pitching in chapter 2.4.

(10) Attend events in your niche and network or even get a booth or speak

Most podcasters choose to market their show online, but you can stand out at networking events and industry trade shows by talking about your podcast in person.

You could pitch for a speaking slot, or get a booth and cover it with podcast art. Make sure to take business cards with links to your show or a QR code that directs people to the right place.

(11) Create and wear a t-shirt that features your show

You can also get t-shirts or other wearables made with your podcast art on either side. I have one for *Books and Travel* and wear it at author events. Lots of people notice it, which gives me a chance to provide them with more details.

(12) Use paid advertising

If you have a budget, then it might be worth paying for advertising. Since podcasts are the best way to market podcasts, you can sometimes get an audio slot on other shows in your niche. You'll need a short audio advert of less than two minutes with a clear call to action, so people can hear your voice and learn more about your show.

You could also consider paid email newsletter lists, or social media advertising like Facebook or Instagram where you can target people who like a certain show (if it's big enough), or those who like podcasting + your niche. You can even specify a particular device, for example, Apple iPhone or Android, which will enable you to link to the most appropriate app.

(13) Submit your show to lists, awards, and competitions

Once your podcast becomes more established, it's likely to be included in lists of various kinds. For example, *The Creative Penn Podcast* often appears in lists of the Best Podcasts for Writers. You can create lists like this on your website or a site like Medium and include your show amongst the others.

There are also competitions and awards that you can submit your show to, for example, The British Podcast Awards, or genre-specific awards like Best Fancast at the Hugo Awards in the sci-fi genre. Just search online for the most up-to-date information in your niche.

(14) Keep producing great content on a consistent schedule

The best marketing is word of mouth — people telling other people about your show. This is more likely to happen if you produce fantastic content on a regular basis for the long term. After all, if your podcast is a habit for hundreds or even thousands of listeners every week and they find it useful, interesting, or entertaining, they will tell others about it. I often ask friends what they're listening to right now, and we share our podcast recommendations just as often as books.

* * *

These are just some ideas for marketing your podcast, but there will always be new opportunities, so keep an eye out for what other podcasters are doing. If you're not happy with the number of subscribers to your show, then there's a lot you can do to aid discoverability. You just have to market as hard as you create!

Questions:

- How will you market your podcast? What ideas resonate with you?

2.18 Re-purpose your podcast content

Once you have a podcast, you can re-purpose that content in other ways, creating new material as well as marketing assets and even other income streams. Not everyone listens to podcasts, so if you have your content available in different ways, you will attract new people into your ecosystem.

Turn your podcast into a pillar article with bonus extras

If you have show notes and a transcript for the podcast, you can flesh that out into a useful resource for your audience. You could provide helpful cheatsheets as a free download or even as part of an email signup. This can become a pillar article on your site, something you can direct people to over time, bringing you more traffic and email signups.

Turn your audio podcast into a video

You can create basic videos for your podcast very easily. Just add an image to your sound file and use a standard program on your computer to turn that into a video. There are also lots of apps that can do this for you, or you can use a premium program. I use Screenflow for the Mac, as I also do video tutorials and other video editing. You could also use Headliner app, which automatically turns podcasts into video.

Upload the video to YouTube or other video-sharing platforms or share snippets on social media.

You can also take this further and prepare more engaging video to attract an audience who prefer to consume visually.

If you do interviews, you could record them in video rather than just audio.

You can see many of my video interviews at:

YouTube.com/thecreativepenn

If you do a solo or chat show, you could **record it as a Facebook Live video and then re-purpose it later into an audio podcast**. I record a monthly live conversation as part of the *Ask ALLi Podcast* for the Alliance of Independent Authors with the founder, Orna Ross. We do an advanced show for independent authors and record it on Facebook Live. The video is used on YouTube and then shared later on an audio podcast feed.

Just search *Ask Alli* on your favorite podcast app for the backlist episodes.

Turn a longer episode into multiple shorter pieces

If you do value-packed longer episodes, as I sometimes do on a particular topic, you could break that down into shorter snippets. Those can be used on social media or turned into videos for easier consumption on platforms that favor short-form content.

Turn your backlist into a paid product

By definition, podcast episodes go out on a feed and are usually free. However, you can remove episodes from the feed later and turn that audio into a paid product. You can even leave it there for free, and some people will still buy if you make it into a useful and easy-to-consume package.

Dan Carlin turns his *Hardcore History* seasons into paid audio products that customers can buy and download from his website. Scott Sigler podcasts his fiction but also sells the audiobook versions.

Use your podcast as the first draft of a book

Brad Barrett and Jonathan Mendonsa, co-hosts of the *Choose FI Podcast* worked with another author, Chris Mamula, to turn their popular financial independence show into a bestselling book, *Choose FI: Your Blueprint to Financial Independence.*

Tim Ferriss, author of *The 4-Hour Work Week*, turned his podcast into a book, *Tools of Titans*, which collated top tips from hundreds of world-class performers.

The *Lore Podcast* about folk-tales with an edge of horror has been turned into a number of books, *Dreadful Places*, *Monstrous Creatures,* and *Wicked Mortals.*

On the fiction side, *Welcome to Night Vale* has been turned into a book series, and Scott Sigler continues to podcast his fiction as part of his writing process.

I've intended to write a travel memoir for years, but it's

hard to make the time when memoir takes a long time to process and shape into a finished book. So I decided to write about my travels, record the episodes and release on my *Books and Travel Podcast*. Over time, I will collect enough material to form the basis of a first draft.

Of course, there is a lot of work needed to turn podcast episodes into a finished book, but it can be an effective way of creating thousands of words toward a future finished product.

Questions:

- What are some ways that you could re-purpose your podcast content?

2.19 The money side of podcasting

An author asked me recently whether the time spent pod-casting is worth it in terms of book sales income. The short answer is no — but podcasting is not just about direct book sales. It is only one part of an ecosystem of creative busi-ness opportunities. In this chapter, I'll explain the multiple streams of income available to podcasters, but first, there is a more fundamental question to consider.

What do you want to achieve with your show?

It's very easy to podcast these days. Pick an app, talk into it and click to publish. Your words will be in the world in seconds — but that doesn't mean anyone will hear it, and it doesn't mean you will make the impact you seek. So what do you want to achieve with your podcast and also with your creative ecosystem?

Your answer to this question will determine how you choose to podcast, and also how you choose to both spend and make money with your show.

If you want to get a podcast out in the world without spend-ing any money; if you're happy to build someone else's brand, give up ownership of your content, give control of your feed to another company, and let them choose how they monetize your show, then go ahead and use the free creation tools that are expanding every day.

If you are an independent creator and you want to build your brand, own your content, and make your own decisions about what companies can advertise in your show, as well as choose the type of business you run, then pay for podcast hosting, invest in your show as an asset, and monetize it in the way that feels right for you.

These are two very different approaches, but you have to think about what you want to achieve with your creative ecosystem for the long term.

My initial goal for *The Creative Penn Podcast* back in 2008 was to network with other creatives, but my website was always a business. I intended to leave my job to become a full-time author entrepreneur, and the podcast was part of that business design.

In 2015, podcasting became a lot more expensive for me in terms of time and hosting costs, and it was only then that I switched to monetizing the show in multiple ways.

> Your podcast can be a business asset that will bring you revenue for the long-term — but only if you design it that way.

Here are some of the ways to make money with your podcast.

(1) Don't expect to make money for at least a year — possibly longer

Yes, you can earn good money as a podcaster and there are some big-name shows that make over US$100,000 per month — but they are not the norm! The vast majority of podcasters, like the vast majority of authors, don't make much money with their shows.

Money cannot be the reason to start a podcast, and there are far easier ways of making an income. You have to love audio and the podcast medium and want to do it for other reasons first. Once you have an audience, you can consider monetization.

You should plan for future income, but don't expect to make tons of cash immediately. This is the same as being an author, blogging or speaking, or anything where you are not paid directly for your time. You have to build the asset first, invest your time and probably some money, and at some point, you may see a return.

So, what is *your* why? Will that carry you through at least a year of investment?

It's hard to see the future when you start, but I would still podcast even if I won the lottery. It is primarily part of my creative body of work and gives me a purpose and a community.

Lindsay Buroker, co-host of the *Six-Figure Author Podcast*, says, "I write science fiction and fantasy and podcast about self-publishing and marketing, so my podcast definitely isn't a funnel to lead people into buying my novels. Now and then, someone will say they bought a book because of the podcast, but I do it more because I enjoy sharing what I learn, and in a way that I can reach a lot of people at once."

(2) Indirect sales and income

"I do *not* think podcasting helps sell books, except for perhaps some of my non-fiction, but that boost is very slight. It *does* direct listeners to my author services (retreats and weekly write-ins), so in that way, I see some profit from it."

Rachael Herron, Author and Podcaster at RachaelHerron.com

Podcasting is a great way to build a personal brand in a niche, to gain expert or even influencer status, and to attract other business opportunities. All these things are indirect benefits of podcasting, because there might be no way for you to track the income as specifically related to your show. It is also cumulative, increasing over time as your reach grows.

Someone might find your podcast and start listening, then months later, might buy your book, support you on Patreon or decide to book you for speaking or coaching. Your show could result in a lot of incoming business and money in your bank account, but since there is no single clickable link to demonstrate direct income as a result of an episode, it is not measurable in the same way that a Facebook ad can directly link to a book sale.

You can, of course, use different links in your podcast, but that can be hard to manage. I use the same links in my podcast call to action as I do everywhere else on the inter-

net: Download my Author Blueprint at TheCreativePenn.
com/blueprint. I get hundreds of signups per week to this
list, but I don't know how many come from the podcast.
I also sell hundreds of books per week, but again, I don't
know which of those sales come as a result of the show.

You can maximize this indirect income in the following
ways:

- Use a **clear call to action** in your intro and outro to
  drive people to your email list so you can continue
  marketing over time

- Talk about your **books, products, services, events,
  webinars, merchandise, affiliate links, consulting,
  and coaching** as a natural part of your show, so
  listeners know what you have available. Be sure to
  use easy to say and remember links.

- Make yourself the main sponsor of the show so that
  listeners get used to a sales message, for example,
  "Today's show is sponsored by my book, *How to
  Write Non-Fiction*, available now in ebook, paperback and audiobook editions."

- Include **buy links in your show notes** and transcript
  so people can click through

All these things assume that you have a business around
your podcast so the show is not your only offering. If you
don't have anything to sell, decide what you intend to offer
at some point and build toward that goal. For more detail,
check out my book, *Business for Authors: How to be an
Author Entrepreneur*.

"My main business is coaching creatives, which happens one deep conversation at a time. It makes a lot of sense for my listeners to hear me talking to inspiring creatives, to get a sense of what it's like to be in a conversation with me. The show has been a great source of new coaching clients, who already have a strong sense of knowing me and relating to my work before we have even met."

Mark McGuinness, Poet, Creative Coach and Host of The 21st Century Creative Podcast, 21stCenturyCreative.fm

(3) Direct sales

If you use trackable links in your episode show notes and transcripts, you will have clear evidence of which links lead to sales.

You can also use **specific promo codes** in your podcast. When the codes are used later for sales, you can track who came through the show. This only works when you control the sales process and is not applicable for book sales on Amazon or other stores where you don't have information on the buyer.

You can **re-purpose and sell older episodes** of your show. For example, Dan Carlin's *Hardcore History* podcast is free to listen to recent episodes, but you can also buy his backlist episodes on specific topics. This works well for topic-specific shows when the content can be collated into these more audiobook-type products. Dan also has **merchandise** like t-shirts and hats, as well as a book, *The End is Always Near*. Check out his site at DanCarlin.com to see the incredible value he offers his listeners and how he monetizes his show.

Some podcasters with a large audience present live recordings of their show and sell tickets for listeners to attend.

(4) Advertising and sponsorship

Paid advertising on podcasts has become much more common, even for smaller shows, so don't think you need to be super-famous to get corporate sponsorship. It's more about having a relationship with a clear audience and then connecting with companies who want to reach those people.

If you're podcasting through a free service, they will allocate the advertisers, and you may (or may not) receive a share of that revenue. But if you're independent, you can choose who you work with.

- Which companies would fit best with your niche?

- Which companies do you already use in your business?

- Who can you authentically recommend?

These questions are important because they give an indication of what marketing might resonate well with your audience. It can be easy enough to get a podcast sponsor, but you will only retain them for the long term if they find it beneficial for their business, too.

Once you have a company in mind, it's worth pitching them for podcast sponsorship. After all, the worst that can happen is that they might say no, but they might say yes, and that's money in your pocket.

If you move in the same circles, and attend the same conferences, **develop relationships within the company.** Find out who the decision-makers are so you know who to talk to. Find out what kind of budget they have and what else they are doing for marketing. Does your podcast fit into their plans?

Prepare your pitch material

You need proof of downloads and evidence of the audience you bring to the company. This is where IAB certification will become increasingly important over time, since it is verifiable in terms of downloads. In contrast, the industry is aware that some companies are inflating numbers for advertising purposes. [Both Libsyn and Blubrry, the services I recommend, are IAB certified.]

In my pitch document, I include download numbers for the last 3-6 months as well as traffic to my website and social media reach, since I share episodes there as well. Downloads increase over time as new listeners will often download shows from the backlist, so sponsors usually get much more than they paid for.

Be clear about what the sponsor will get for their money

My sponsors get a mid-roll audio slot as well as an image and a link in the show notes, plus social media sharing. They can provide an audio file of up to two minutes, or I will do an ad read with my own experience and the benefits of the service.

Use industry-standard rates — or decide your own

This is your show and your brand, and it is valuable. Don't undersell yourself. But of course, when you're starting out, you are likely to start small!

Mid-roll sponsorship slots can range from $10 - $100 or more per 1,000 CPM (cost per mille, or downloads). You get to decide your rates if you are an independent pod-caster, or you can work with an advertising company like Midroll.com.

You should have at least 1,000 downloads per episode con-sistently over a six-month-period before even considering advertising.

If you want to keep your advertisers for the long term, you will need to prepare statistics every period to show evidence of continuing downloads.

Book advertisers for more than one slot

Aim for 6-12 episodes, if possible, to minimize the amount of invoicing, reporting and chasing for money you have to do.

You may get pitched for podcast sponsorship by other companies as your show grows in influence. I've had many of these over the years, and some have very generous offers. But if you cannot authentically support that company and you don't use it yourself or think it would be truly useful for your audience, then it is unlikely to last, and you may damage the trust you have with your tribe. I turn away the vast majority of pitches for podcast sponsorship as they are not appropriate for my audience. I only work with companies I believe in and use myself.

YouTube can be a form of advertising revenue, and you can make some money by activating ads there, even if you have an audio-only show. However, the revenue is tiny for most shows, and it's far better to consider more targeted advertising that you control. I have advertising on some videos on YouTube.com/thecreativepenn but not on episodes with a sponsor.

(5) Patreon, subscription, and community funding

We live in a wonderful world where many people want to support creators who provide value. That support may come from buying a book, leaving a review, or sharing on social media, or by giving money to the creator through services like Patreon, a fantastic way to give a small amount per month to fund continued creativity.

My podcast is free to download and listen to on pretty much every podcast app, but a small proportion of wonderful listeners also choose to pay $2 - $10 a month on Patreon because they find the show valuable and want to help pay for my time and encourage me to continue. Once you understand how long it takes to podcast as per chapter 2.15, you'll also see how valuable this support can be!

Patreon and other community support only works if you have an existing audience, and you already provide value. It's also a slow-growth form of income, and supporters will drop in and out as their preferences change, so the money goes up and down every month.

You need to provide Patron-only rewards, so make sure these are scalable and resonate with your audience. I do a Patron-only monthly Q&A audio on writing, publishing, book marketing, and making a living with your writing. New patrons can also access the backlist Q&A episodes, so they get a lot of audio extras.

It makes sense to produce audio rewards when you have an audio product, but Patreon also has a list of other options, including behind-the-scenes extras, physical merchandise, fan participation, and more.

I am truly grateful for my Patreon supporters, not only for their financial contribution but also for their continued enthusiasm for the show. It definitely helps me return to the microphone when I feel like it's all a bit much!

> If you'd like to support *The Creative Penn Podcast* or see what I offer, go to:
>
> Patreon.com/thecreativepenn

Some podcasters take the community funded model further with subscription-only shows. Sam Harris of the *Making Sense* podcast switched to a subscriber model, offering full-length episodes instead of snippets, extra conversations and advance tickets for live events to his supporters.

(6) Charge guests to appear on your show

This is not something I do right now, but it is happening on shows that are big enough to command an audience worth paying for with guests who have a marketing budget. There is an application process for the show, and the guest has to commit to a fee of several thousand dollars in order to appear.

This might sound outrageous to some, but podcasting takes time and money, especially as an independent, and it is essentially free marketing for guests. If a podcaster has invested time and money for years building up an audience and has hundreds of pitches per month for their show, then introducing an appearance or access fee is not so unreasonable. It is similar to advertising, but it's more for an individual than a company.

Check out an example at Eofire.com/guest and also one podcaster's open letter on why he charges podcast guests:

TheCreativePenn.com/chargepodcastguests

The P&L (Profit and Loss) of a podcast

Money flows in and out of a business at different times, and an understanding of cash flow is essential if you want to monetize.

You will start by spending time and money on your show. You might have to buy equipment as well as services to create, distribute and market your podcast, plus you will need to put in the hours to learn new skills, interview guests, prepare content, and more.

Once your audience is big enough to start making money from your show, the income will be a trickle at first. If you persist, you might make a profit, but that will depend on how you choose to monetize as well as consistency over time and how well you serve your audience.

John Lee Dumas, podcaster at *Entrepreneur on Fire,* shares an income report with a breakdown of his multiple streams of income. He has podcast sponsorship and advertising, but he also has sales of courses, books, mastermind programs, affiliate income, and more. You can also see his expenses per month. Check it out at: Eofire.com/income

Questions:

- What do you want to achieve with your podcast? What will make it worthwhile even if you don't make any money?

- Do you want to be an independent podcaster or work within a network where they control content and advertising?

- What are some ways you could monetize immediately?

- How could you monetize in the future if your listenership grows?

- If you want to do corporate advertising, what are some of the companies that might be interested in your niche? How will you approach them?

- How could you offer value to a community on Patreon? What might you offer for reward levels?

- Have you considered the P&L of your podcast? How will the timing of cash flow affect your business?

Part 3: Voice technologies

3.1 Overview

"Every decade or so, there is a tectonic shift in how people interact with technology … The latest technological disruption is happening, and it promises to be one of the most sizable and momentous that the world has ever seen. We are entering the era of voice computing."

James Vlahos, Talk to Me: Amazon, Google, Apple and the Race for Voice-Controlled AI

There's more to the voice ecosystem than just podcasting and audiobooks, and in this section, I'll outline some of the main technologies that might be useful to authors. It must be noted that voice technology changes all the time, with more developments announced almost every day. This section will give you a place to start and the language to begin your own investigations.

As an overview, we will cover:

1) **Speech to text.** Authors can use dictation to write the first draft of books, articles, podcast episodes, and more.

2) **Text to speech.** Authors can use automated text readers to proof manuscripts as well as create and edit audio products with emerging speech tools.

3) **Voice assistants and smart speakers.** As readers and listeners begin to use voice search for information, inspiration, and entertainment online, authors need to ensure their books can be found through these new discovery mechanisms. There are also

opportunities for storytelling through this more interactive medium.

(4) **Artificial Intelligence (AI) and the future of voice.** There are many applications of AI to voice technologies, including the development of human-level voice for audiobook narration, and the impact of AI tools on copyright law.

3.2 Speech to text: Dictation

"In the next 10 years, if you're not embracing voice, you will be behind in the same way as if you don't have a smartphone right now. You're missing out on a lot of technological help."

Scott Baker, The Writer's Guide to Training Your Dragon

When most people say they are 'writing' a book, they tend to mean typing with their fingers on a computer keyboard. Before typewriters, people only thought about writing by hand, with a pen or a quill. Before that, it might have been carving symbols onto stone.

But think about the end result.

A book is a **mode of communication between your brain and the brain of a reader.** How it gets there is not so important.

Speech-to-text technology is critical for those who cannot write because of physical challenges, illness, or learning difficulties, but it can also be a healthier and more productive way of writing for authors in general.

A number of famous authors wrote, or still write, with dictation. John Milton of *Paradise Lost*, Dan Brown, Henry James, Barbara Cartland, the incredibly prolific romance author, and Winston Churchill. You probably couldn't get two more different people than Barbara Cartland and Winston Churchill!

When Terry Pratchett, author of the *Discworld* fantasy series, couldn't write anymore because of early-onset Alzheimer's, he moved into dictation. I've written parts of a number of my books with dictation so, clearly, it can be an effective mode of creation.

Why consider dictation for your writing?

Writing speed and stamina improves with dictation. It's much faster to speak words than it is to type them, especially if you can get out of your own way and stop self-censoring. I can type around 2,000-3,000 words in a first draft writing session of two hours, but with dictation, I can get up to 5,000 words in the same period.

There is definitely a trade-off. Until you can improve at dictation, your words won't be as polished as typing them at a slower pace. You'll need to do an editing pass. But sometimes just getting the rough draft down as fast as possible is useful, and then you can go back and edit later. The trade-off reduces over time as you improve your process.

Another benefit is **increased creativity**. Many writers suffer from perfectionism when typing. They obsessively correct and retype the same paragraph over and over again because a first draft for a beginning writer is not going to be fantastic. If you keep rewriting at this early stage, you may never finish the book, but dictating bypasses that critical voice because no one expects speech to be perfect, and you know you can fix it later.

Dictation is healthier. Many people get into dictation because they suffer from Repetitive Strain Injury or some kind of pain that impacts their ability to type. Or they realize they need to make a change to the writer's sedentary life and move more. Even if you don't need dictation now, you may need it later, especially if you want to make a living with your writing for the long term. Consider dictation as a way to future-proof your career as a writer. Hopefully, you can avoid health issues, but if you do ever suffer from them, you will have other ways of creating.

If dictation is so amazing, why isn't everyone doing it?

Here are some of the most common issues, and I know these very well, because I have said all of these things myself!

- I'm used to typing. I don't have the right kind of brain for dictation.

- I don't want to say the punctuation out loud. It will disrupt my flow.

- I write in public, so I can't dictate.

- I have a difficult accent which will make it impossible for the speech-to-text software.

- I write fantasy books with weird names, so I can't possibly dictate.

- I don't know how to set it up technically.

- I can't spare the time to learn how to dictate.

- I can't afford the software.

These are all valid concerns, but if dictation can make your writing process more effective and healthier, then it's worth considering.

I've found that dictation really helps to get the first draft down so I can move into editing. I don't use it for every book, but when I have, it's made the process faster. I still resisted it, though.

Here's my journal entry on the first day I tried dictation.

> "I'm very self-conscious. I'm worried that I won't be able to find the words. I'm so used to typing and creating through my fingers that doing it with my voice feels strange.
>
> But **I learned to type with my fingers, so why can't I learn to type with my words?** I just have to practice. Something will shift in my mind at some point, and it will just work.
>
> This should make me a healthier author and also someone who writes faster. Authors who use dictation are writing incredibly fast. That's what I want. I want to write stories faster, as I have so many in my mind that I want to get into the world."

Here's my journal entry *after* the first session:

> "It felt like the words were really bad and the story clunky and poor, but actually when the transcript was done and I lightly edited it, **it wasn't as bad as I thought it would be.** A classic case of critical voice. I need to ignore this when I'm dictating.

I definitely need to plan more before I speak, which will save time overall in both dictation and editing. I thought I would find the punctuation difficult, but it has been easier than expected. There are only a few commands that you use regularly, and dialogue is the worst, but you get into a rhythm with that. It also gives you a pause between each speaker to consider what they might say next. So perhaps it is a blessing in disguise."

I hope these journal entries help you in terms of addressing your fears before you start. Once you get into it, you realize that it's not that bad after all. You just have to try it yourself.

There are different methods of dictation.

(1) Speech to text in real-time

There are lots of programs for speech-to-text now, and most computers have a speech to text or dictation mode for word processing programs.

Nuance Dragon is the most well-known software, and they have an app, Dragon Anywhere, for mobile use, but it can be pricey. Try these other options for starters:

- Open Google Docs in the Chrome Browser. Click Tools -> Voice Typing

- On the Mac, use Edit -> Start Dictation

- On the PC, hold down the Windows key and press H to trigger the dictation toolbar. (This may vary with your version of Windows.)

Once dictation is enabled, speak directly into the computer, and words will appear on the screen. Accuracy will improve with a separate microphone, but you can start with just your usual computer setup. Edit as you dictate or fix it up later.

You can use voice commands to do a whole lot more, and if you do have health issues and you can't use your arms or hands much, then that's probably the mode you want to use. Personally, I don't like to look at the screen as I dictate, as it engages my critical voice.

(2) Dictate now, transcribe later

This is my preferred method of dictation. I record the audio and then get it transcribed. Again, there are a lot of options for this, and the price of transcription is coming down fast because of artificial intelligence so look around for the latest options. Here are a few:

- If you have Dragon, upload the MP3 in Transcription mode to produce a .txt file

- If you prefer a human, use Speechpad.com or Rev. com

- AI transcription is cheaper and improving all the time, so check out services like Descript.com, Trint. com or Otter.ai

Once you get your transcription back, just a few minutes later if you're using software or AI services, you can do a first pass edit to fix up any punctuation or typos. I copy and paste my transcribed files into Scrivener, lightly edit with one pass and then properly edit after the first draft is complete.

Technical setup

As above, you don't have to spend any money. You can use free apps on your phone to record and free software like Google Docs for dictation, so don't let fear of technical setup or expense get in the way of trying it. But of course, if you want to improve accuracy, there are a few things you can do.

The quality of your microphone makes a difference, as does making sure to record in a quiet environment. If the software can understand your voice more easily, the transcription will obviously be better.

For first draft recording, I use a handheld Sony ICD-PX333 MP3 recorder which you can find at:

TheCreativePenn.com/sony

I hold it near my mouth and use the Pause button in between thoughts. You can also use a Lavalier (or lav) lapel microphone that plugs into your phone if you want to walk and talk.

When recording directly into my computer, I use a Blue Yeti microphone, which I also use for my podcast and audiobooks, which you can find at: TheCreativePenn.com/blueyeti

Technology changes fast and prices continue to drop, so search online for the best services and products for your situation.

Tips from writers who dictate

Kevin J. Anderson is an incredibly productive author with hundreds of books published, most of which he dictated while hiking.

> "The biggest advice that I would give for you and other writers to get started with dictation is don't try to write that way. **The best way is to start to do notes or brainstorming.** Take your recorder and go for a walk. It's almost like free association.
>
> When you're starting out, don't think that you have to do full sentences. Maybe **use your first round of dictation to plot and plan and get notes down.** That can be a really good way to get started with dictation."

Kevin has a book on dictation, *On Being a Dictator: Using Dictation to be a Better Writer.*

Monica Leonelle's *Dictate Your Book* has a lot of great tips on dictation and when I interviewed her, she noted,

> "Dragon thinks very differently than we do. **We think in words, but Dragon thinks in phrases.** So think about what you're going to say and then speak it with confidence. This makes punctuation easier too."

This is a really good tip and why I use the pause button when dictating. Dragon and other speech recognition software use placement and order because **language is not just about an individual word, it's about context**. This is really important. When you're typing, you think about each word, whereas when you're dictating, you need to speak in phrases.

Christopher Downing, author of *Fool Proof Dictation*, stresses the importance of warming up and cyclical dictation exercises that lead up to the main dictation session. He also stresses quality and a cleaner first draft with this cycling approach.

> "If we can get high words and yet, at the same time, warm up the craft side of our brain where we can dictate a decent sentence, or a somewhat complicated sentence that's written beautifully, I think that is better in the end."

> You can listen to all these interviews and find more options for dictation at:

> ThecreativePenn.com/dictation

All these books and interviews are useful, but at some point, you need to try dictation yourself. Open one of the free options and record a few paragraphs. Pick some of your own text or take a book off the shelf and read it aloud. You might find that dictation is the tool that transforms your writing process.

Questions:

- Why might you consider dictation? How might it help your writing?

- What's stopping you from dictating? How can you work through those issues in order to try it?

- What method of dictation might work for you?

- What tools do you need to get started?

3.3 Text to speech

Text-to-speech software has long been used for accessibility purposes, but now the applications are expanding into other areas.

Check your written work by using a text-to-speech reader

There comes a point in the writing process where you can't see your own words anymore. Editing becomes almost impossible because you cannot be objective. At this point, it can help to read the manuscript out loud, or you could use text-to-speech software to do it for you.

Options include NaturalReaders.com and TTSReader.com.

AI voices

Artificial voices have come a long way from the super-robotic to the almost human. Google Cloud Text-To-Speech has 180 voices across 30+ languages and variants, Amazon Polly has "dozens of lifelike voices across a variety of languages," and IBM Watson enables your system to speak like a human in multiple languages and dialects.

These services are cloud software-as-a-service, so they can be used for customer service applications, chatbots, and integration with natural language processing models like sentiment data analysis.

Authors can use AI voices to turn text into narration, but at the time of writing, you cannot publish audiobooks with an AI voice — but you can produce podcasts or add audio to your blog with services like Speechkit.io.

> If you'd like to turn your book into a podcast with an AI voice through Amazon Polly, check out this tutorial by Makoto Tokudome at:
>
> TheCreativePenn.com/PollyBookToPodcast

Voice synthesis

You may have seen some of the deep fake videos posted online by Instagram user @bill_posters_uk. They include Donald Trump, Mark Zuckerberg, Kim Kardashian, and Boris Johnson, among others, pronouncing things they would never say in real life. It's not just the video that is faked — it's also the sound of their voices.

In December 2019, Amazon announced the release of the Samuel L. Jackson Alexa Skill. Just say, "Alexa, introduce me to Samuel L. Jackson," choose explicit or clean language options and then ask him some questions.

The responses are not necessarily a recording. As technology blog, *The Verge,* reported, "Instead of relying entirely on prerecorded phrases, the Samuel L. Jackson voice is powered in part by Amazon's neural text-to-speech model. It's like a lightweight deepfake, but the actor obviously gave his permission to stand in for Alexa's standard voice."

It's not just celebrities who can create synthesized voices — podcasters and audiobook narrators can do it, too. In fact, anyone with enough data to train a voice algorithm can work with one of the voice-synthesis companies to create a voice.

Descript.com allows creators to edit audio by editing the text transcript, as well as automatically removing filler words from the recording by identifying words like 'um' in the transcription. It also has an OverDub feature which allows a podcaster to correct audio by typing, powered by Lyrebird AI, a company specializing in voice synthesis that Descript acquired in 2019.

Since I have many hours of voice recording, Descript.com made me my first Voice Double in late 2019. Over time, as I record more and add more data to the algorithm, the quality will improve, and hopefully, I will be able to license my voice to narrate other people's audiobooks or play a part in a podcast drama.

You can hear the various iterations at:

TheCreativePenn.com/voicedouble

Questions:

- Are there any situations where you might find text-to-speech applications useful?

3.4 Voice assistants, smart speakers and devices

It's important to consider the context for audio consumption and interaction to understand growth in the medium and how you can potentially take advantage of the opportunities ahead. Accessibility and inclusivity are fantastic reasons for voice and audio development, but the technologies have now transitioned to the mainstream, so they will improve at a faster rate.

Of course, not everyone has experience with all these devices, so let's start with definitions.

Voice assistants

These are automated software applications that respond to voice commands in order to answer questions, perform tasks and/or interact with the user in other ways. The most well-known are Google Assistant, Amazon Alexa, Siri for the Apple ecosystem, and Cortana for Microsoft, although there are many more on less dominant platforms. They exist across multiple devices in an ecosystem, for example, Siri is in my Apple Watch, my iPhone, my MacBook Pro, and our Apple HomePod.

Each voice assistant has a wake word or phrase, like "Hey Google," and then you ask a question or use words to perform a task. The assistant will answer out loud and/or perform the task. For example, I'm cooking while wearing my Apple Watch, and my hands are full. I can say, "Hey

Siri, set a timer for 20 minutes." Or I'm out of lentils, so I say, "Alexa, add lentils to my shopping list."

There are lots of voice assistants, and it's likely there will be many more over time as different companies deploy them, so it's best to think of them like apps for your phone. You are likely to use specific assistants for separate tasks, rather than a single one for everything, and some are better at things than others. For example, I use Google Assistant for questions when I want a specific answer. I used to type them into the Google Search bar on my phone, but now I say "Hey Google," and ask out loud. This shift in search behavior is driving change in the search algorithms as covered in chapter 3.5 on optimizing for voice.

I also use Siri for tasks on my Apple Watch and Alexa to play music or an audiobook when I'm home alone and want some company.

Smart speakers

Since the most common voice search is for music, it makes sense that the first iteration of devices were smart speakers. These include the Amazon Echo, Apple HomePod, and the Google Home Speaker, but also third-party speakers that use the core ecosystems. For example, the Sonos smart speaker has both Alexa and Google Voice control.

Smart speakers are particularly interesting for authors because they can be used to listen to audiobooks and podcasts, as well as music and radio.

Voice-activated devices

The various voice assistants are now included in different devices and activated by voice. There are devices for the home, for example, a thermostat to control temperature, a smart plug to turn on your lights or a camera for security.

You can integrate assistants into your car, so you don't even have to touch the control panel to play your favorite tunes or continue listening to your audiobook or podcast.

It's not just audio devices that use voice activation. Many devices also have a screen, for example, the Echo Show has video, and you can use Siri with Apple TV.

Since the voice assistants are software applications that can be used in different ways, it's likely that many more devices will come onto the market with voice activation in the future.

Some examples of voice in action

If all this sounds too technical, and you're wondering why this shift is so important, consider these more personal examples.

Bob is retired and lives alone. His daughter lives overseas with her family. He doesn't sleep so well and often wakes in the early hours. His eyesight isn't good, but he loves reading history books. "Alexa, play Stalingrad by Anthony Beevor." Later, he might call his daughter through his Echo Show so he can see the grandkids.

Asha gets up early and dresses for the gym. She puts on her Apple watch. "Hey Siri, what's the weather outside?" When

Siri says it's going to rain later, Asha grabs her raincoat and walks to the gym, listening to a podcast on her AirPods.

Jasmine is three. When she gets home from pre-school, her mum is too busy to play but doesn't want her to watch TV. Her dad is away with his work, but she can listen to him read a story he recorded specially for her. "Hey Google, talk to My Storytime." Jasmine listens to her dad while she makes a castle with her building blocks.

Celine and Fei are watching *The Crown* on Netflix and arguing over whether it portrays the truth about Princess Alice. Celine keeps one eye on the TV while she asks her phone, "Hey Google, who was Princess Alice of Battenberg?"

Rishi has Type 2 diabetes that worsened because, in the past, he would forget to take his meds. At 9 am, Alexa says, "It's time to take your medication."

Janet arrives in Madrid and wants to speak with her local host. "Hey Google, help me speak Spanish." The assistant translates the conversation in real-time.

These are just some examples of people in typical situations using voice to interact with devices, where in the past, they might have typed something or physically pressed a button. This doesn't even touch on the business or government applications of voice, and barely scratches the surface of what is available now, let alone what is coming.

The integration of voice into healthcare is particularly interesting, as it is already showing benefits. *Business Insider* reported in late 2019 that voice technology could "shrink costs associated with poor medication adherence," as well as "reduce physician's administrative burden," and eliminate transcription costs.

In mid-2019, the National Health Service (NHS) in the UK teamed up with Amazon Alexa to provide information on specific illnesses. The health secretary, Matt Hancock, said, "Technology like this is a great example of how people can access reliable, world-leading NHS advice from the comfort of their home, reducing the pressure on our hardworking GPs and pharmacists."

In terms of creative storytelling, companies like Tellables are creating voice-led experiences specifically for smart speakers as well as games for children to learn through story. Google Assistant's My Storytime allows parents to record stories remotely that the children can listen to later, inspired by a real US military family. You can even go on a Choose Your Own Adventure® story through Alexa, making choices at each stage to impact the plot and the ending.

This chapter is just an introduction to the possibilities ahead. For more detail, I recommend reading *Talk to Me: Amazon, Google, Apple and the Race for Voice-Controlled AI* by James Vlahos.

Since publishing the book, James has gone on to launch Hereafter.ai, which creates conversational avatars with the voices of loved ones. He produced a 'Dadbot' when his father was diagnosed with terminal lung cancer and now aims to preserve voices for others.

Whatever you think about this development, it is a glimpse into the possible future of voice.

"As Google CEO Sundar Pichai put it in a letter to stockholders, 'The next big step will be for the very concept of the 'device' to fade away.' With voice, computers are to be ubiquitous rather than discrete, invisible rather than embodied. Digital intelligence will be everywhere, like the air we breathe."

James Vlahos, Talk to Me: Amazon, Google, Apple and the Race for Voice-Controlled AI

Questions:

- In what situations have you experienced or observed people interacting with voice assistants?

- Consider what might be possible. Then go check whether it already exists.

3.5 Optimizing for voice

If more people are searching by voice, and more readers are consuming by audio, then how do we make sure our books can be found? Here are some ways that you can optimize for the voice ecosystem.

(1) Publish in audiobook format

If a reader searches by voice and prefers the audio medium and your book is not available in audio, you are basically invisible. Sure, they might discover you by other means and put your book on a list to look at later, but if they can't listen to a sample and buy immediately, you may have lost that sale.

In the next decade, audio will become ubiquitous, like ebooks in the 2010s, always available as a format choice. Chapter 3.6 covers how the costs will come down even further to make this possible.

(2) Create audio for marketing purposes

If a reader prefers audio, they often discover books through podcasting and audio-related means. I don't read blogs anymore and get the vast majority of my non-fiction book recommendations through podcast interviews. If I hear an author I resonate with, or someone speaking intelligently on a topic I am interested in, I am likely to check out their book.

In mid-2019, Google started indexing podcast episodes, so a search query will return text-based answers, video, and now audio as separate responses. If you want to be found, you need to be available in audio.

(3) Publish wide so you can be discovered on every voice platform

If your books are exclusively on Amazon, they will not be found by someone who uses the Google or Apple voice ecosystem. According to Statcounter, 75% of mobile phones worldwide use the Google Android operating system, which means that Google Assistant, Google Podcasts and Google Play are default apps on those devices.

Of course, the various other audiobook apps can be used on different devices, but don't assume that one ecosystem is dominant globally just because it is most common in your country.

Those three steps will be more than enough for most authors, but if you want to go further, then read on.

(4) Optimize your website for voice search

If you're an author with a business that is wider than just books and an extensive website, or you use content marketing, this section might be relevant for you.

Voice search differs from typing. When you type a search query into Google, you expect to have several pages of results. You might use a few keywords and then scan the first few pages for the most appropriate site, or even open several pages in order to go deeper into the topic.

But if you speak a query into Google Assistant, you won't get pages of answers. You will get whatever Google determines is the best answer spoken aloud. Someone who asks a question while driving does not want to have to look at a screen for the answer.

But these are not the only voice options. It is increasingly common to use voice search on a mobile device that returns text-based results. I do this on my phone all the time, and it will increase with more widespread wearable technology like smartwatches. The user is likely to speak in longer, more specific phrases, or even full sentences as they would do with another person. This significantly changes the search terms and results.

In late October 2019, my website traffic at TheCreative-Penn.com dropped as Google implemented the BERT update to their search algorithm. After more than a decade of organic traffic, it seemed that quality material from an authority source around specific keywords was no longer enough. This has given me an insight into what the shift to voice will mean for many businesses, as I needed to make some changes.

Previous Search Engine Optimization (SEO) guidelines were about creating lots of content around the main key-words, but the BERT update focuses on natural language, the kind you might use when searching by voice. It is also more about **search intent and providing the best user experience for a specific question.**

It is now important to create super-useful content around specific questions and long-tail keyword phrases instead of broader keywords, although, of course, quality material and an authority site still matter.

As Neil Patel, an SEO expert, stated, "It's not necessarily about creating a really long page that talks about 50 different things that's 10,000 words long. It's more about answering a searcher's question as quick as possible and providing as much value compared to the competition."

You can also use Featured Snippets within your website which come with standard plugins for WordPress like Yoast with other solutions for different site software.

(5) Feeling technical? Check out Alexa Skills and Google Template Actions

You can create Skills or Actions that relate to the content of your book with specific wake words to activate them. There are developer toolkits for the Alexa and Google ecosystems, and if you're technical and interested, you can build your own, or work with freelancers.

However, think of these in the same way as books or apps in a crowded store. People have to discover them somehow, so make sure to factor marketing into the equation.

* * *

There are many possibilities for voice optimization, but start with the basics before you expand into other areas.

Questions:

- Are your books available in audio on every voice ecosystem?

- Are you creating free audio content like podcast episodes or interviews for marketing?

- How can someone who chooses voice-first find you?

3.6 Artificial Intelligence (AI) and the future of voice

"The adjacent possible is a kind of shadow future, hovering on the edges of the present state of things, a map of all the ways in which the present can reinvent itself."

*Steven Johnson, The Genius of the
Tinkerer in the Wall Street Journal*

Possibilities are expanding fast, so it's challenging to keep up to date with the many changes in the voice and audio space. This chapter is just a glimpse of what might be coming and its potential impact for creators. Of course, the future is hard to predict, so these are just my thoughts on a shifting audio landscape.

Voice synthesis and AI narrators

At the time of writing, it is not possible to publish an audiobook with an AI narrator on the leading audiobook platforms. However, this will likely change in the coming years. Firstly, because the market demand is growing ever faster and there are not enough narrators to produce the audio version of all content in English, let alone in every language or dialect. While there will always be a place for high-production-value human narration, many listeners just want to consume audio versions of written content on their preferred platforms and are happy to have an AI voice narrate it.

In developing markets, this is even more urgent. At Frankfurt Book Fair Audio Summit 2019, one of the speakers from Latin America said they would look at AI voices to produce audio content faster because they couldn't possibly manage the demand with only human narration.

Secondly, AI voices are becoming more human-like. Google's Tacotron 2, Microsoft's FastSpeech, Amazon's Alexa and Polly all have voices that, in some cases, are indistinguishable from humans. Chinese companies Baidu and iFlytek are even further ahead with voice development, with *Forbes* reporting in May 2019 that it now takes Baidu's Deep Voice only 3.7 seconds of audio to clone a voice.

Companies like Descript (who bought voice-synthesis specialists Lyrebird in 2019) and Deepzen.io are working on narration with intonation and emotion.

Chinese news agency *Xinhua* has several AI news anchors, digital avatars with the realistic voices of the humans they were modeled on. These were created by the search engine company, Sogou, which announced in August 2019 that they were developing artificial intelligence lookalikes to read popular novels in the voice of the author.

In December 2019, Amazon Alexa introduced Samuel L Jackson as a Skill. As reported in *The Guardian*, "The Jackson feature will allow users of Alexa-enabled devices to interact with an AI version of the actor developed using the company's neural text-to-speech technology. Jackson is not the first celebrity to feature on Alexa, but previous celebrity voice features have relied upon pre-recorded audio."

The fact that this is not pre-recorded audio is important because it means that Jackson's voice has been (presumably) licensed to speak words he has not physically said. It is a voice synth.

At some point in the 2020s, audiobook retailers will likely accept AI-narrated audiobooks, and podcasts by AI voices will be indistinguishable from humans, so what are the potential impacts for consumers, authors and creators, narrators and the publishing industry?

Impact on consumers

From a reader and listener perspective, AI voices will expand the market considerably because it will be easier and cheaper to produce audiobooks, podcasts, and other audio content. If every book and piece of written text is available in audio, more people will consume in that format. There are a lot of books I want to listen to that are not available in audio right now, and availability will inevitably mean more sales.

AI voices will also enable more options for listeners, as it should be possible to choose the narrator per book, or switch voices to someone you resonate with. I listen to a lot of business and finance books, and most are narrated by American male voices. I'd love to be able to choose a British female voice instead. Another listener might prefer Indian-English, or Nigerian-English. Why not have every possibility in every language and dialect with AI voices? We connect with people we know, like and trust, and voice is clearly a part of that. Would audiobook readers consume even more books if they could listen in a voice they preferred?

A renaissance in audio content will require new forms of discovery that index audio and serve consumer intent. The audiobook platforms have a certain level of discoverability built-in, but it's still hard to find audiobooks unless you know what you're looking for. As listeners consume more audio, expect AI-driven tools to learn preferences in more detail and surface content the user might enjoy in the same way that Spotify does for tailored music and podcast preferences.

Impact on authors and creators

AI voices will expand the potential for audio creation. Many creatives are writing audio dramas, radio plays, podcast fiction, narrative non-fiction audio, and other forms of storytelling for voice. If you want to produce that content in audio format with humans, it's expensive and time-consuming to get voice talent into studios, record, and then edit them together into a narrative. But creation with AI voices, or text-to-speech generated from licensed voices, will speed up the process and make it a lot cheaper.

For authors, the big question is — who owns and controls your audiobook rights? Have you already licensed them, and for what formats? How valuable will those audio rights be in a global, digital, AI-voice-driven future? Are you able to take advantage of the opportunities that may arise?

Impact on narrators

There will always be a place for high-quality, experienced human narrators, but the audio market will likely expand into other options over time. People buy different versions of books to serve different needs, and in the same way, they will likely purchase different versions of audiobooks.

The AI-narrated version might be the price of an ebook or mass-market paperback, while the human-narrated, artisan-produced version would be at a premium price. If listeners want a physical representation of the experience, this might even bring back vinyl or tapes for audiobooks in the same way that it has done for the music industry.

Mass-market audio is likely to be AI-narrated — but many listeners will want books in the voices of their favorite narrators. Voice licensing to the AI-audio producers will enable voice talent to monetize without doing the work of narration, bringing costs down for rights-holders, delivering great content, and producing income for narrators. Smart contracts on blockchain technology will enable tracking through the digital audio ecosystem, and voice talent will receive micro-payments for voice usage across audiobooks, podcasts, and text-to-speech reading of other content.

I narrate my own non-fiction audiobooks, and as a creator with several podcasts, I have skin in this voice game. I've increased the rate of my self-narrated audio to produce more data which can be used to train an AI voice. I fully intend to license it once the technology is available.

> You can listen to the development of my Voice Double produced by Descript.com at:
>
> TheCreativePenn.com/voicedouble

I intend to create a voice brand for audiobook narration and to become a recognizable voice that creators and producers want to license for their projects.

For narrators, the big question is — how ready are you for this shift? Do you own and control enough recordings of your voice to train an AI? The majority of narrators don't own their recordings, because copyright is assigned at the contract stage.

Are you willing to license your voice to creative audio projects where you are not physically involved? Are you ready to shift to other ways of working in order to bring in new revenue streams?

Impact on the publishing industry

The publishing industry is about licensing and control of intellectual property that is turned into books and associated products that consumers want to buy. Yes, of course, it is also about art and culture, beautiful literature, education, inspiration, and entertainment — but without money, the business doesn't work.

Publishing contracts generally include audiobook rights as standard these days, but will those clauses hold up to new ways of audio creation with AI? Audiobook production, until now, has been based upon creating one finished product with a specific narrator or set of narrators, but how will that change if a consumer can select a voice or a language?

The limits of audiobook copyright law were tested in mid-2019 when Audible introduced a Captions feature allowing consumers to read along with audiobooks. Audible argued that the text was generated by AI and not from the text of the book itself, so it did not breach the licensing agreement. A number of large publishers sued Audible, citing a violation of copyright. The dispute was resolved in early 2020, but these types of agreements will need to be hammered out as technology changes.

It's likely that copyright law will have to shift to incorporate the possible changes ahead, perhaps with new subsidiary rights that cover the prospect of multiple productions from a single primary work.

Of course, all of the above assumes human creation of the original work. But copyright law is also being challenged by AI generation of written text as well as music, art and more.

In January 2020, a Chinese court ruled that an article generated by an AI was protected by copyright, as reported by Venture Beat. The article was written by Dreamwriter, automated software created by Tencent, one of China's largest technology companies.

In the same week, two other announcements marked a significant shift in the potential of AI to create. Google announced their Reformer AI language model that can process the entirety of novels, expanding the possibilities of natural language processing. The Guardian reported on the use of AI in Hollywood, with one company ScriptBook developing Deepstory, a screenwriting AI. They noted, "Within five years we'll have scripts written by AI that you would think are better than human writing."

The publishing industry is made up of many wonderful people who love authors and books, but it is also a business. If AI systems can write books that satisfy readers and AI narrators can read them aloud for a fraction of the cost of working with human authors and narrators, then why wouldn't a publisher use those systems for at least some of their product lines?

Privacy, ethical issues and more

It must be noted that there are privacy, ethical, and copyright law issues inherent in many of these voice technologies and implications for the people who currently make a living in these areas.

These issues are beyond the scope of this book, but my hope is that more authors, creators, narrators, and publishing industry professionals will engage with the tech community to ensure our diverse voices are heard in the many discussions to come. Too many are dismissing these developments as irrelevant or so far ahead that the status quo will remain for the foreseeable future. But AI technology is accelerating faster than ever. Those who want to thrive in the years to come will see the change coming and surf the wave rather than drown in it.

The future is almost here.
How do we keep up?

It was challenging to write this part of the book because technology changes every day, and this section is essentially outdated as soon as I finish writing. But I wanted to give a flavor of the world we live in right now and a glimpse of what might be on the horizon.

If you want to stay up to date on voice technologies, follow VoiceBot.ai, and you can also check out #voicefirst on Twitter for news and updates. There are also a number of voice-related conferences and I share news about the impact of AI in my futurist segment on *The Creative Penn Podcast* with highlights collected at:

TheCreativePenn.com/future

Questions:

- What are you excited about in terms of potential for future voice technology? How can you take advantage of what might come?

- What concerns you? How might you position yourself to participate in the conversation and protect your lifestyle in the years ahead?

- How will you stay up to date with the changes in voice technology?

Conclusion

"When we want meaningful emotional experience,
we go to the storyteller."

Robert McKee, Story

We have come full circle, back to the fireside where we have always told each other stories. But now we can take our voices so much further, creating new experiences for listeners all over the world through technologies that continue to advance.

There will only be more opportunities to create as the global demand for audio grows, and as people seek connection with others, voice may be the most effective medium to reach readers in the years ahead.

Technology will continue to shift, but there will always be a desire for entertainment, information, and inspiration, and audio is a fantastic way to deliver it. I hope you found the book useful and I wish you all the best for your audio journey ahead.

Need more help on your author journey?

Sign up for my *free* Author 2.0 Blueprint and email series, and receive useful information on writing, publishing, book marketing, and making a living with your writing:

www.TheCreativePenn.com/blueprint

* * *

Love podcasts? Join me every Monday for The Creative Penn Podcast where I talk about writing, publishing, book marketing and the author business. Available on your favorite podcast app.

Find the backlist episodes at:

www.TheCreativePenn.com/podcast

Appendix 1: Chapter notes

Chapter notes, references and resources are included in the Appendices and on the download page at:

TheCreativePenn.com/audiobookdownload

Why audio? Why now?

The Audio Publishers Association reports 7 years of double-digit revenue growth for audiobooks in the USA - Publishingperspectives.com/2019/07/audio-publishers-association-survey-nearly-1-billion-in-2018-sales/

The Independent reports that audiobook sales are predicted to overtake ebook sales in the UK in 2020 - Independent.co.uk/life-style/audiobook-sales-ebook-kindle-uk-deloitte-2020-a9229266.html

Edison Research Infinite Dial Report 2019: Edisonresearch.com/infinite-dial-2019

Audiobooks are the fastest growing segment of the publishing market. Publishing Perspectives Publishingperspectives.com/2019/07/audio-publishers-association-survey-nearly-1-billion-in-2018-sales/

Marketing Rebellion: The Most Human Company Wins - Mark W Schaefer

The audio-first mindset

BBC - What does your accent say about you? Bbc.com/future/article/20180307-what-does-your-accent-say-about-you

1.1 Types of audiobooks

Who Am I, Again? - Lenny Henry

Born a Crime: Stories from a South African Childhood - Trevor Noah

Infected - Scott Sigler

On Writing: A Memoir of the Craft - Stephen King

Women Who Run with the Wolves: Myths and Stories of the Wild Woman Archetype - Clarissa Pinkola Estés

Big Magic: Creative Living Beyond Fear - Elizabeth Gilbert

Audible Originals - *War of the Worlds, Alien: Sea of Sorrows*, and Jane Austen's *Emma*

Six Degrees of Assassination, a 10-part audio drama - MJ Arlidge

Underland: A Deep Time Journey - Robert Macfarlane

Brand New Ancients: A Poem - Kate Tempest

1.2 Writing, adapting and editing for audio

The Guide to Publishing Audiobooks: How to Produce and Sell an Audiobook - Jessica Kaye

Natural Reader text to speech: Naturalreaders.com

Writing for Audio First. Interview with Jules Horne - TheCreativePenn.com/audiofirst

Writing for Audio Books: Audio-First for Flow and Impact - Jules Horne

Pitch Audible Originals at Audible.com/ep/audible-pitch

1.3 Intellectual property considerations

Closing the Deal on your Terms: Agents, Contracts and Other Considerations - Kristine Kathryn Rusch

The Copyright Handbook: What Every Writer Needs to Know - Stephen Fishman

How Authors Sell Publishing Rights: Sell your Book to Film, TV, Translation and Other Rights Buyers - Orna Ross and Helen Sedwick

The Guide to Publishing Audiobooks: How to Produce and Sell an Audiobook - Jessica Kaye

CNN article on Taylor Swift and other musicians who lose control of their master recordings - edition.cnn.com/2019/07/01/business/taylor-swift-rights-trnd/index.html

1.4 Your options for audiobook publishing and distribution

The Martian - Andy Weir Andyweirauthor.com

Podium Publishing - Podiumpublishing.com

The Martian: how the audiobook hit rocketed to film glory - TheGuardian.com/books/2016/jan/27/the-martian-audiobook-hit-rocketed-oscars-glory

Audio Publishers Association - Audiopub.org

Audie Awards - Audiopub.org/winners

The Guide to Publishing Audiobooks: How to Produce and Sell an Audiobook - Jessica Kaye

1.5 How to find and work with a professional narrator

Audiobook services that will help you find a narrator: ACX.com and FindawayVoices.com

The Guide to Publishing Audiobooks: How to Produce and Sell an Audiobook - Jessica Kaye

Veronica Giguere, audiobook narrator and voice talent - VoicesByVeronica.com

ARKANE thriller series audiobooks - JFPenn.com/audio

1.6 Reasons to narrate your own audiobook

Productivity for Authors: Find Time to Write, Organize your Author Life, and Decide What Really Matters - Joanna Penn

Examples of authors who have narrated their own audiobooks:

- *A Thousand Fiendish Angels* – J.F.Penn

- *Infected* – Scott Sigler

- *The Graveyard Book* – Neil Gaiman

- *Shades of Milk and Honey* – Mary Robinette Kowal

- *On Writing: A Memoir of the Craft* – Stephen King

1.7 Audiobook narration tips

This is a Voice: 99 Exercises to Train, Project and Harness the Power of your Voice - Jeremy Fisher and Gillyanne Kayes

Storyteller: How to be an Audiobook Narrator by Lorelei King and Ali Muirden

Audiobook narration tips. Interview with Lorelei King: TheCreativePenn.com/storyteller

Audiobook narration tips: Interview with Sean Pratt: TheCreativePenn.com/sean

Narrate and Record your own Audiobook: A Simplified Guide - M.L.Buchman iAnnotate.com - App to read, markup and share PDFs that I use for audiobook narration

1.8 Recording studio options

VocalBoothToGo.com - Sound blankets and mobile audio set-up

*Narrate and Record your own Audiobook:
A Simplified Guide* - M.L.Buchman

My home studio set-up with links to equipment:
TheCreativePenn.com/homestudio

1.9 Audiobook recording, editing and production

ACX technical audio submission requirements: Audible-acx.custhelp.com

Findaway Voices requirements for assets: my.findawayvoices.com/docs/Technical_Requirements_for_Assets.pdf

Dropbox.com for sharing files

Audio recording and editing software:

- Amadeus Pro - Hairersoft.com/pro.html

- Audacity - Audacityteam.org

- Avid Pro Tools - Avid.com/pro-tools

- Adobe Audition -
  Adobe.com/products/audition.html

Narrate and Record your own Audiobook: A Simplified Guide - M.L.Buchman

Find freelancers to help with the audiobook production process:

- Ask at your local studio sound engineer. Even if they usually work with musicians or local radio, they will likely be able to help with audiobook production.

- Upwork.com

- PeoplePerHour.com

- Audio Book Publishers Association - Audiopub.org

1.10 How to self-publish an audiobook

Recommended sites for self-publishing audio: ACX.com and FindawayVoices.com

Audio Book Publishers Association - Audiopub.org

KWL Audio. Submit directly at Kobo.com/writinglife

Chirp Books for audiobook deals - ChirpBooks.com

CDBaby: cdbaby.com/make-discs.aspx

1.12 How do audiobook readers discover audiobooks?

BookBub deals on ebooks - BookBub.com

BookBub Chirp audiobook promotions - chirpbooks.com

Amazon Audible Matchmaker for finding audio editions

of ebooks - Amazon.com/hz/audible/matchmaker

The Body: A Guide for Occupants - Bill Bryson

Audible on Alexa - Audible.com/ep/audible-on-alexa

1.13 How to market audiobooks

Amazon Author Central. Email the help team to link editions of your books together per country store: authorcentral.amazon.com

Books2Read.com - Create one shareable link to all editions

Books2Read.com/makealiving - Links for the ebook and audiobook editions for How to Make a Living with your Writing as an example

Landing page for my audiobooks for authors - TheCreativePenn.com/audio

My Audible Author pages are:

- Joanna Penn for non-fiction: Audible.com/author/Joanna-Penn/B002BM8ICW

- J.F.Penn for thrillers and dark fantasy: Audible.com/author/J-F-Penn/B00AVLL4WG

Headliner for audiograms - headliner.app

Canva.com - Create shareable images of the correct size for social media

Soundcloud.com - Create shareable audio samples

Audiogram from Productivity for Authors on Twitter at TheCreativePenn.com/audiogram

Soundcloud audiobook trailer for Valley of Dry Bones at Soundcloud.com/jfpenn/valley-of-dry-bones

Sample chapter of Successful Self-Publishing on YouTube at TheCreativePenn.com/samplechapter

Amazon Advertising - Accessible through kdp.amazon. com dashboard for advertising ebooks which can be linked to the audiobook edition

Tutorial for building a website: TheCreativePenn.com/ authorwebsite

Tutorial for building an email list: TheCreativePenn.com/ setup-email-list

BookFunnel.com - Easily distribute ebooks and also audio snippets to multiple devices so you don't have to manage customer service

ACX promotional giveaway codes - blog.acx. com/2019/05/09/get-cookin-with-new-and-improved-promo-codes

Authors Direct giveaway codes from Findaway Voices: Authors-direct.com/giveaway-codes

Pay per checkout model for libraries: Medium.com/ findaway-voices/library-audiobook-marketing-what-you-need-to-know-58aa5cd90b3

Amazon Audible Matchmaker for finding audio editions of ebooks - Amazon.com/hz/audible/matchmaker

BookBub deals on ebooks - BookBub.com

BookBub Chirp audiobook promotions - chirpbooks.com

AudiobookBoom.com enables you to reach a list of audiobook listeners. Provide review codes and some of the listeners may leave a review which can help sales.

Audiofile Magazine has options for audiobook reviews and advertising - audiofilemagazine.com

The Audio Publishers Association has promotional opportunities and also lists resources, reviewers and more on their site at Audiopub.org

YouTube.com - Upload audio snippets with static image

Audio Publishers Association survey 2019 reported that 55% of audiobook listeners in the USA had also listened to a podcast in the last month - Audiopub.org/uploads/pdf/Consumer-Survey-Press-Release-2019-FINAL.pdf

Generate QR codes - qr-code-generator.com

1.14 The money side of audiobooks

Closing the Deal ... on Your Terms: Agents, Contracts and Other Considerations - Kristine Kathryn Rusch

The Guide to Publishing Audiobooks: How to Produce and Sell an Audiobook - Jessica Kaye.

ACX royalty details - Audible-acx.custhelp.com/app/browse/c/3529

ACX bounty referral program - Acx.com/help/bounty-referral-program/UEF9JUCH9AZEKA4

FindawayVoices royalty details - blog.findawayvoices.com/author-royalties-with-findaway-voices

Payhip for direct sales - Payhip.com

Shopify for direct sales - Shopify.com

Amazon Audible Matchmaker for finding audio editions
of ebooks - Amazon.com/hz/audible/matchmaker

PART 2: Podcasting

2.1 Why podcasting is important for authors

Google announced in August 2019 that they would
index podcast episodes (not just shows) - TheVerge.
com/2019/8/8/20759394/google-podcast-episodes-
search-results-transcriber

*Make Noise: A Creator's Guide to Podcasting and Great
Audio Storytelling* - Eric Nuzum

The 21st Century Creative Podcast:
Lateralaction.com/21stcenturycreative

The Six-Figure Author Podcast: 6figureauthors.com

My call to action for the Author Blueprint -
TheCreativePenn.com/blueprint

2.3 Types of podcasts

Seth Godin, Podcasting is the new blogging -
seths.blog/2018/10/podcasting-is-the-new-blogging-2

Sleepwalkers Podcast - iheart.com/podcast/1119-
sleepwalkers-30880104

Writing Excuses Podcast - writingexcuses.com

Serial Podcast - SerialPodcast.org

The Joe Rogan Experience - podcasts.joerogan.net

The Creative Penn Podcast -
TheCreativePenn.com/podcast

Books and Travel Podcast - BooksAndTravel.page/listen

Dan Carlin's Hardcore History Podcast -
DanCarlin.com/hardcore-history-series

9 Ways that Artificial Intelligence with Disrupt Authors
and Publishing in the Next Decade - TheCreativePenn.
com/2019/07/01/ai-disruption-publishing-authors

Escape, Reinvention, Curiosity, Challenge.
Why Travel? - BooksAndTravel.page/why-i-travel

Wondery's Dirty John Podcast:
Wondery.com/shows/dirty-john

This American Life - ThisAmericanLife.org

Podiobooks, now Scribl.com, for self-publishing audiobooks and ebooks with different pricing models

7th Son - JC Hutchins

Infected - Scott Sigler

Welcome to Night Vale Podcast -
WelcomeToNightvale.com

2.4 How to research and pitch podcasters

Popular podcast platforms - Apple Podcasts, Google Podcasts, Spotify or Stitcher

Happiness, Anxiety and Writing with Lisa M Lilly. Listen at TheCreativePenn.com/lisa

Living on the Edge: Greenland with Christoffer Petersen BooksAndTravel.page/greenland

2.6 Should you start your own podcast?

Podcasting is the new blogging. Seth Godin's blog: Seths.blog/2018/10/podcasting-is-the-new-blogging-2

Make Noise: A Creator's Guide to Podcasting and Great Audio Storytelling - Eric Nuzum

Stark Reflections on Writing and Publishing - StarkReflections.ca

How Do You Write - RachaelHerron.com

Writing Excuses Podcast - writingexcuses.com

I Should Be Writing Podcast - Murverse.com/subscribe-to-podcasts/isbw

2.8 Intellectual property considerations for podcasts

Alliance of Independent Authors www.TheCreativePenn.com/alliance

Electronic Frontier Foundation's Legal Guide to Blogging
www.eff.org/bloggers

Audiojungle.net - Royalty free music and audio tracks
with different kinds of licenses depending on your needs.

Incompetech.com - Creative Commons music created by
Kevin MacLeod

BigStockPhoto.com - Royalty free stock photo site

Unsplash.com - Creative Commons images

Podcasting Legal Guide -
wiki.creativecommons.org/wiki/Podcasting_Legal_Guide

2.9 Podcasting equipment and software ***HERE**

My first podcast episode I'm March 2009
- TheCreativePenn.com/episode1

Options for recording:

- Skype.com and add-ons
  Ecamm.com/mac/callrecorder

- Zoom.us

- Zencastr.com

- Cleanfeed.net

Equipment I use and recommend:

- Ring light 'for make-up' for video interviews

- VocalBoothToGo.com - Sound blankets and mobile audio set-up

- Blue Yeti microphone: www.TheCreativePenn.com/blueyeti

- Pop filter

- ATR2100 microphone

- Zoom H4n for recording live interviews

Editing software:

- **Audacity.** For Mac and Windows. audacityteam.org

- **Amadeus Pro.** Mac only. Hairersoft.com/pro.html

- **Screenflow.** Mac only. You can do video editing with Screenflow so if you're producing a video podcast, you can use this for both video and audio exports. Telestream.net/screenflow

- Use Camtasia for the PC. Techsmith.com/video-editor.html

- If you want to get serious about audio editing, check out **Adobe Audition** or **Avid Pro Tools**.

2.11 How to be a great podcast host

- *Make Noise: A Creator's Guide to Podcasting and Great Audio Storytelling* - Eric Nuzum

- Calendly.com for booking guests across time zones

2.12 Podcast distribution

Libsyn.com - You are in control of your podcasting hosting, distribution and monetisation

Blubrry.com - The most flexible tools for podcasting

My affiliate link for Blubrry - TheCreativePenn.com/podcasthost

Blubrry PowerPress Plugin for WordPress - create.blubrry.com/resources/powerpress

Blubrry IAB Certified Professional Podcast Statistics - create.blubrry.com/resources/podcast-media-download-statistics

Amazon S3 scalable cloud hosting - aws.amazon.com

The Podcast Host for more technical questions: ThePodcastHost.com

Podcast Host Academy - my recommended course if you want to learn about podcasting - TheCreativePenn.com/podcastacademy

My YouTube channel: YouTube.com/thecreativepenn

2.13 Show notes and transcripts

AI created transcription: Descript.com, Otter.ai, Rev.com

Human transcription. This will be more exact but it will usually cost around US$1 for one minute of audio. Services include speechpad.com and rev.com, both of which I have used personally and can recommend.

Social Warfare Plugin for WordPress - warfareplugins.com

Canva.com for creating shareable images at appropriate sizes

BigStockPhoto.com for royalty-free photos

Unsplash.com for creative commons images

2.14 Collaboration and freelancers

Writing Excuses Podcast

The Writer's Well Podcast with J. Thorn and Rachael Herron

The Author Life Podcast with J. Thorn

How Do You Write? Podcast with Rachael Herron

Dropbox.com for sharing files

Google Sheets - docs.google.com/spreadsheets

Find freelancers at: Upwork.com, PeoplePerHour.com or Fiverr.com

Big Gay Fiction Podcast and *Big Gay Author Podcast*

Frolic Podcast Network - frolic.media/podcasts

2.15 Podcast workflow and tools

Calendly.com - calendar scheduling across time zones

Skype.com for internet interviewing and recording

Descript.com for transcript and audio snippets

Speechpad.com for human transcription

WordPress site for blog post - tutorial here: TheCreative-Penn.com/authorwebsite

Amadeus Pro for recording intro or solo episodes. Can also be used for audio editing, although Dan uses Pro Tools.

Dropbox.com for file sharing

Auphonic.com for audio levelling and adding metadata

Blubrry PowerPress plugin for distributing file - TheCreativePenn.com/podcasthost

Canva.com for creating shareable images

Screenflow for creating video for YouTube

Patreon.com for sponsorship by patrons

Buffer.com for scheduling social media

Headliner.app for audiogram creation

Turn the Page: Mental Health Podcast - Turningthepage.info/podcast-listen-mental-health

2.16 How to launch a podcast

If you need help with your website or email list, check out my tutorial at: TheCreativePenn.com/authorwebsite

How to hit Apple iTunes Podcast New and Noteworthy - castos.com/itunes-new-and-noteworthy/

2.17 How to market a podcast

You can find my podcast home pages at TheCreativePenn.com/podcast and BooksAndTravel.page/listen

Canva.com for creating shareable images

Headliner.app or Wavve.com for audiograms

Audiogram from the Books and Travel Podcast on Twitter at TheCreativePenn.com/podcastaudiogram

Social Warfare Plugin for WordPress - warfareplugins.com

Tutorial for setting up an email list: TheCreativePenn.com/setup-email-list

2.18 Repurpose your podcast content

Screenflow for the Mac - Telestream.net/screenflow

My video interviews at YouTube.com/thecreativepenn

Ask ALLi Podcast for the Alliance of Independent Authors with the founder, Orna Ross. https://selfpublishingadvice.org/self-publishing-advice-podcast/

Dan Carlin turns his *Hardcore History* seasons into paid audio products DanCarlin.com

Scott Sigler podcasts his fiction but also sells the audiobook versions. ScottSigler.com

Choose FI Podcast and book - ChooseFI.com

Tools of Titans - Tim Ferriss collated top tips from hundreds of world-class performers from interviews on Tim's show

Lore Podcast and books LorePodcast.com

Welcome to Night Vale has been turned into a book series WelcomeToNightvale.com

2.19 The money side of podcasting

Six-Figure Author Podcast with Lindsay Buroker, Joe Lallo, and Andrea Pearson

Rachael Herron, Author and Podcaster RachaelHerron.com

My call to action: Download my Author Blueprint at TheCreativePenn.com/blueprint

Business for Authors: How to be an Author Entrepreneur - Joanna Penn

The 21st Century Creative Podcast - 21stCenturyCreative.fm

Dan Carlin's *Hardcore History* podcast DanCarlin.com

IAB certification for Blubrry statistics - create.blubrry. com/resources/podcast-media-download-statistics

Midroll.com - for advertising

Patreon.com - for community support

If you'd like to support *The Creative Penn Podcast* or see what I offer, go to: Patreon.com/thecreativepenn

Charging guests to come on the show. Check out an example at Eofire.com/guest and also one podcaster's open letter on why he charges podcast guests: TheCreativePenn.com/chargepodcastguests

John Lee Dumas, podcaster at *Entrepreneur on Fire* shares an income report with a breakdown of his multiple streams of income and expenses. Check it out at: Eofire.com/income

Part 3: Voice technologies

3.1 Overview

Talk to Me: Amazon, Google, Apple and the Race for Voice-Controlled AI - James Vlahos

3.2 Speech to text: Dictation

Nuance Dragon and Dragon Anywhere: Nuance.com

Free dictation

- Open Google Docs in the Chrome Browser.
  Click Tools -> Voice Typing

- On the Mac, use Edit -> Start Dictation

- On the PC, hold down the Windows key and press
  H to trigger the dictation toolbar. (This may vary
  with your version of Windows.)

Transcription

- If you have Dragon, upload the MP3 in
  Transcription mode to produce a .txt file

- If you prefer a human, use Speechpad.com
  or Rev.com

- AI transcription is cheaper and improving all the
  time, so check out services like Descript.com,
  Trint.com or Otter.ai

For first draft recording, I use a handheld Sony ICD-PX333 MP3 recorder which you can find at: TheCreativePenn.com/sony

When recording directly into my computer, I use a Blue Yeti microphone, which I also use for my podcast and audiobooks: TheCreativePenn.com/blueyeti

The Writer's Guide to Training Your Dragon: Using Speech Recognition Software to Dictate your Book and Supercharge your Writing Workflow - Scott Baker

On Being a Dictator: Using Dictation to be a Better Writer - Kevin J Anderson and Martin L. Shoemaker

Dictate Your Book: How to Write Your Book Faster, Better, and Smarter - Monica Leonelle

Fool Proof Dictation: A Non-Nonsense System for Effective and Rewarding Dictation - Christopher Downing

Interviews on dictation and more options for dictation at TheCreativePenn.com/dictation

3.3 Text to Speech

Text-to-speech software:

- NaturalReaders.com

- TTSReader.com

Google Cloud Text to Speech: cloud.google.com/text-to-speech

IBM Watson Text to Speech: Ibm.com/watson/services/text-to-speech

Amazon Polly: aws.amazon.com/polly

Speechkit for turning text into audio for your website:
Speechkit.io

Deep fakes on Instagram -
Instagram.com/bill_posters_uk

Descript.com - Overdub and Voice Double

My voice double iterations at
TheCreativePenn.com/voicedouble

Tutorial on how to turn your book into a
podcast with Amazon Polly -
TheCreativePenn.com/PollyBookToPodcast

December 2019, Amazon announced the release of the
Samuel L. Jackson Alexa Skill
TheVerge.com/2019/12/12/21013145/amazon-echo-alexa-
samuel-l-jackson-celebrity-voice-now-available-price

3.4 Voice assistants, smart speakers and devices

Talk to Me: Amazon, Google, Apple and the Race for Voice-Controlled AI - James Vlahos

Business Insider report on healthcare - businessinsider.
in/science/news/voice-assistants-in-healthcare-an-
inside-look-at-3-emerging-voice-use-cases-healthcare-
providers-can-deploy-to-cut-costs-build-loyalty-and-
drive-revenue/articleshow/72499316.cms

The Guardian. NHS teams up with Amazon to bring Alexa to patients - https://www.theguardian.com/society/2019/jul/10/nhs-teams-up-with-amazon-to-bring-alexa-to-patients

Voicebot.ai New Google Assistant App helps parents read to kids from far away: voicebot.ai/2019/11/24/new-google-assistant-app-helps-parents-read-to-kids-from-far-away

Tellables voice app on Alexa for stories: Tellables.com/author-tips

Hereafter.ai - enabling conversations with loved ones after they die

Google Real-time translation on your phone: blog.google/products/assistant/interpreter-mode-brings-real-time-translation-your-phone

3.5 Optimizing for voice

Google now indexing podcast episodes: TheVerge.com/2019/8/8/20759394/google-podcast-episodes-search-results-transcriber

How Google's BERT update will affect content marketing: NeilPatel.com/blog/bert-google

Statcounter, 75% of mobile phones worldwide use the Google Android operating system: gs.statcounter.com/os-market-share/mobile/worldwide

Develop for Google Assistant: developers.google.com/assistant/templates

Develop for Amazon Alexa: blueprints.amazon.com

Voice Summit conference: Voicesummit.ai

Use Featured Snippets within your website which come with standard plugins for WordPress like Yoast

3.6 AI and the future of voice

Steven Johnson, The Genius of the Tinkerer in the Wall Street Journal: wsj.com/articles/SB1000142405274870398 93045755037301011860838

Descript (which owns Lyrebird) for voice synthesis: Descript.com

Microsoft's FastSpeech AI speeds up realistic voices generation: Venturebeat.com/2019/12/11/microsofts-fastspeech-ai-speeds-up-realistic-voices-generation

Google's voice-generating AI is now indistinguishable from humans: qz.com/1165775/googles-voice-generating-ai-is-now-indistinguishable-from-humans

Artificial Intelligence can now copy your voice: What does that mean for humans? Forbes.com/sites/bernardmarr/2019/05/06/artificial-intelligence-can-now-copy-your-voice-what-does-that-mean-for-humans/#523d482372a2

Chinese news agency adds AI anchors to its broadcast team: Engadget.com/2018/11/08/chinese-news-agency-ai-anchors

AI reads books out loud in authors' voices: bbc.co.uk/news/technology-49329650

Amazon announced the release of the Samuel L. Jackson Alexa Skill TheVerge.com/2019/12/12/21013145/ amazon-echo-alexa-samuel-l-jackson-celebrity-voice-now-available-price

We've been warned about AI and music for over 50 years, but no one's prepared. On AI and copyright. TheVerge. com/2019/4/17/18299563/ai-algorithm-music-law-copyright-human

Chinese court rules AI-written article is protected by copyright. Venturebeat.com/2020/01/10/chinese-court-rules-ai-written-article-is-protected-by-copyright

Google's AI language model Reformer can process the entirety of novels. Venturebeat.com/2020/01/16/googles-ai-language-model-reformer-can-process-the-entirety-of-novels/

'It's a war between technology and a donkey' - how AI is shaking up Hollywood. TheGuardian.com/film/2020/jan/16/its-a-war-between-technology-and-a-donkey-how-ai-is-shaking-up-hollywood

AI system 'should be recognised as inventor' bbc.co.uk/news/technology-49191645

Listen to the development of my Voice Double produced by Descript.com: TheCreativePenn.com/voicedouble

Audible introduced a Captions feature allowing consumers to read along with audiobooks - TheBookseller.com/news/audible-launches-captions-text-feature-us-1040276

US Patent and Trademark Office Seeking Comment on Impact of AI on Creative Works - aitrends.com/ai-in-government/us-patent-and-trademark-office-seeking-comment-on-impact-of-ai-on-creative-works

I share news about the impact of AI in my futurist segment on The Creative Penn Podcast with highlights collected at TheCreativePenn.com/future

Appendix 2: Bibliography

This Bibliography is included on the download page at:

TheCreativePenn.com/audiobookdownload

Books to help with your audio journey

Closing the Deal on your Terms: Agents, Contracts and Other Considerations - Kristine Kathryn Rusch

Dictate Your Book: How to Write Your Book Faster, Better, and Smarter - Monica Leonelle

Fool Proof Dictation: A Non-Nonsense System for Effective and Rewarding Dictation - Christopher Downing

How Authors Sell Publishing Rights: Sell your Book to Film, TV, Translation and Other Rights Buyers - Orna Ross and Helen Sedwick

Make Noise: A Creator's Guide to Podcasting and Great Audio Storytelling - Eric Nuzum

Narrate and Record your own Audiobook: A Simplified Guide - M.L.Buchman

On Being a Dictator: Using Dictation to be a Better Writer - Kevin J Anderson and Martin L. Shoemaker

Storyteller: How to be an Audiobook Narrator by Lorelei King and Ali Muirden

Talk to Me: Amazon, Google, Apple and the Race for Voice-Controlled AI - James Vlahos

The Copyright Handbook: What Every Writer Needs to Know - Stephen Fishman

The Guide to Publishing Audiobooks: How to Produce and Sell an Audiobook - Jessica Kaye

The Writer's Guide to Training Your Dragon: Using Speech Recognition Software to Dictate your Book and Supercharge your Writing Workflow - Scott Baker

This is a Voice: 99 Exercises to Train, Project and Harness the Power of your Voice - Jeremy Fisher and Gillyanne Kayes

Writing for Audiobooks: Audio-First for Flow and Impact - Jules Horne

Other recommended books and audiobooks

7th Son - JC Hutchins

A Thousand Fiendish Angels – J.F.Penn

Audible Originals - *War of the Worlds, Alien: Sea of Sorrows*, and Jane Austen's *Emma*

Big Magic: Creative Living Beyond Fear - Elizabeth Gilbert

Born a Crime: Stories from a South African Childhood - Trevor Noah

Brand New Ancients: A Poem - Kate Tempest

Business for Authors: How to be an Author Entrepreneur - Joanna Penn

Infected - Scott Sigler

Marketing Rebellion: The Most Human Company Wins - Mark W Schaefer

On Writing: A Memoir of the Craft - Stephen King

Productivity for Authors: Find Time to Write, Organize your Author Life, and Decide What Really Matters - Joanna Penn

Shades of Milk and Honey – Mary Robinette Kowal

Six Degrees of Assassination, a 10-part audio drama - MJ Arlidge

Story: Substance, Structure, Style and the Principles of Screenwriting - Robert McKee

The Body: A Guide for Occupants - Bill Bryson

The Graveyard Book – Neil Gaiman

Underland: A Deep Time Journey - Robert Macfarlane

Who Am I, Again? - Lenny Henry

Women Who Run with the Wolves: Myths and Stories of the Wild Woman Archetype - Clarissa Pinkola Estés

World War Z - Max Brooks

Appendix 3:
List of podcasts

This list is included on the download page at:

TheCreativePenn.com/audiobookdownload

Akimbo Podcast with Seth Godin - Akimbo.link

Ask ALLi Podcast with Orna Ross. Advanced Salon co-hosted monthly with Joanna Penn. selfpublishingadvice. org/self-publishing-advice-podcast

Big Gay Fiction Podcast and Big Gay Author Podcast - jeffandwill.com

Books and Travel Podcast - BooksAndTravel.page/listen

Choose FI Podcast - ChooseFI.com

Dan Carlin's Hardcore History Podcast - DanCarlin.com/ hardcore-history-series

How Do You Write? - RachaelHerron.com

I Should Be Writing Podcast - Murverse.com/subscribe-to-podcasts/isbw

Lore Podcast - LorePodcast.com

Serial Podcast - SerialPodcast.org

Sleepwalkers Podcast - iheart.com/podcast/1119-sleepwalkers-30880104

Stark Reflections on Writing and Publishing - StarkReflections.ca

The 21st Century Creative Podcast: 21stCenturyCreative.fm

The Author Life Podcast - TheAuthorLife.com

The Creative Penn Podcast - TheCreativePenn.com/podcast

The Joe Rogan Experience - podcasts.joerogan.net

The Six-Figure Author Podcast - 6figureauthors.com

The Writer's Well Podcast - TheWritersWell.org

This American Life - ThisAmericanLife.org

Turn the Page: Mental Health Podcast - Turningthepage.info/podcast-listen-mental-health

Welcome to Night Vale Podcast - WelcomeToNightvale.com

Writing Excuses Podcast - writingexcuses.com

Wondery's Dirty John Podcast: Wondery.com/shows/dirty-john

Appendix 4:
Consolidated Question list

You can download these questions on the resource page at:

TheCreativePenn.com/audiobookdownload

The audio-first ecosystem

- What is your audio behavior like right now? How has it changed over time?

- What are some examples of the audio ecosystem that you have experienced yourself or noticed in others? What devices do people use around you? What situations do people listen in?

- How can you widen your perspective to include a global, digital, audio-first consumer?

The audio mindset

- What is stopping you from doing audio?

- How can you shift your mindset to embrace the possibilities of the audio ecosystem?

1.1 Types of audiobooks

- What are the different types of audiobook?

- Where might your work fit into the ecosystem?

- Go to your preferred audiobook store online and sample some of the different types of audiobooks to see what you enjoy. You can sample for free, so it's worth trying a broad range.

1.2 Writing, adapting and editing for audio

- How much adaptation will your book need for audio?

- Why is editing and adapting your work a good idea?

- What are some of the things to consider specifically for fiction?

- What are some of the things to consider specifically for non-fiction?

- What are the possibilities for audio-first writing?

1.3 Intellectual property considerations for audiobooks

- Do you own the subsidiary rights for your book? If you have signed a publishing deal, did that contract include audiobook rights? For which territories and in what format?

- Has the publisher exploited those rights and produced an audiobook or are they just sitting on those rights, in which case you might be able to get them back?

- Do you have a contract with your book cover designer that also includes the audiobook cover? Do you have the rights to use a similar design? Have you ensured your contracts cover the copyright for your book cover designs?

- Do you have a contract with your audiobook narrator and/or producer? Have you been assigned the copyright for the production files?

1.4 Your options for audiobook publishing and distribution

- If you want to license your audio rights, do you have proven sales or a reason that a publisher might want those rights?

1.5 How to find and work with a professional narrator

- What kind of voice do you have in mind for your book?

- How will you find the right narrator?

- How long is your book? How many finished hours of audio will that result in? How much might the narration cost? What rate can you afford for your book?

- What kind of contract will you arrange with your narrator?

- How will you work successfully with your narrator to ensure happiness and success on both sides?

- How will you deal with the QA process?

1.6 Reasons to narrate your own audiobook

- Why might you consider narrating your own audiobook/s?

- How do you feel about someone whose voice you like? What attributes do you ascribe to them? Do you connect more to that person because of their voice?

- Do you have the time, budget, and attitude to invest in learning about self-narration?

- What might be your first project?

1.7 Audiobook narration tips

- How confident are you at reading or performing your written work? What can you do to increase your confidence?

- What will you do if you make a mistake during narration?

- How can you make sure that you maintain energy and a personal connection to the listener while recording?

- How will you prepare yourself and your environment?

- What can you do to reduce extraneous noise?

- Record yourself narrating a piece of your work. Listen back for any noises in the recording. What do you notice?

- If you're hiring a professional studio, what can you do to make sure you get the most out of your time?

1.8 Recording studio options

- What will you use for your recording studio? Why are you making this choice?

1.9 Audiobook recording, editing and production

- What software will you use for recording and editing your files?

- How will you manage your files so you don't lose any work?

- Are you interested in learning the technical side of sound engineering, or do you want to outsource the mastering and production of your files?

1.10 How to self-publish an audiobook

- What are the different options for self-publishing an audiobook? What are the pros and cons for each?

- What would suit your project right now, and how might that change in the future?

1.11 How long does an audiobook take to produce?

- How long will it take for the production of your audiobook?

- What are some of the aspects that might delay your audiobook?

- How will you time the releases of your other editions so you can market the audiobook simultaneously?

1.12 How do audiobook readers discover audiobooks?

- If you listen to audiobooks right now, how do you discover what to listen to next? Ask your friends and family for a wider response.

1.13 How to market audiobooks

- What are some of the ways you could market your audiobook? Note down any quick wins you can achieve in the next month as well as a plan for long-term marketing.

1.14 The money side of audiobooks

- How does the money work if you license your rights?

- How does the money work if you independently publish?

- What are the pros and cons of each for your situation?

2.1 Why podcasting is important for authors

- Why is podcasting important for authors? What are some of the benefits that you find most interesting?

2.3 Types of podcasts

- What are the different types of podcasts?

- Try a few episodes of each, so you understand the possibilities. What do you like or dislike about the different types?

2.4 How to research and pitch podcasters

- What potential niches could you target for your book? Think topics, theme, settings and your own interests.

- What shows do you currently listen to that resonate with your topic?

- Make a list of 15-20 other podcasts you could pitch in your niche and list them in order of importance

- Find out about each host and their audience. What can you offer that would be useful?

- Craft your first pitch for a podcast interview. Does it follow the recommendations as outlined?

- How will you deal with success or rejection?

2.5 How to be a great podcast guest

- Have you researched the host and audience? Do you know how best to serve them?

- Have you prepared your technical setup and environment for the best recording experience?

- Have you prepared talking points?

- How will you ensure that the audience remembers how you made them feel?

- How will you make sure that you can bring your energy?

- How will you make sure the conversation is natural?

- What is your call to action? Have you said it out loud to check that your link is easy to say?

- What will you do after the interview?

- What if the interview goes badly? How will you make sure it's better next time?

2.6 Should you start your own podcast?

- What is your why?

- Are you ready to learn new skills? Do you have the time and budget?

- Are you prepared to put yourself out there?

- Who is the show for? What's in it for them?

- Is the niche big enough? Is there potential future growth in your niche or demographic? What evidence do you have for thinking that way?

- Can you be consistent with production?

- What would make podcasting worth it for you?

2.7 Podcast prerequisites

- Do you know your market? What are the top shows in your niche? What are the second-tier shows? What do you like and dislike about them?

- What specific audience are you going to serve? What do they want to know? How do you already fit into that community?

- What will the name of your show be? What ideas do you have for your sub-title and description?

- How long will the show be? How often will you publish?

- Have you organized your artwork?

- Have you made an initial content plan? Do you have enough ideas for an ongoing show?

2.8 Intellectual property considerations for podcasts

- What do you need to consider around intellectual property for your podcast?

- How will you source music for your show?

- How will you find artwork?

- What will you need to consider around interviews and working with other people?

2.9 Podcasting equipment and software

- What equipment and software do you need right now in order to get started?

- What might you consider investing in later?

- What skills do you need to practice?

2.10 Podcast structure

- What are the different segments that you enjoy on your favorite podcasts? What might be effective for your audience?

- What material will be evergreen, and what will be newsworthy about your show? What will keep people coming back?

- Have you scripted and recorded your intro and outro?

2.11 How to be a great podcast host

- Make a list of 10 people you'd like to interview. Do your research on them and craft a pitch asking them to come on your show.

- How will you prepare for the interview in order to make it a good experience for your guest?

- How will you make sure the conversation goes smoothly and is useful for your audience as well as pleasant for your guest?

- How will you handle it if things go wrong?

2.12 Podcast distribution

- What do you need to consider around distribution for your podcast? What are the pros and cons of paying for hosting?

- Have you researched the different services available? What would work best for your situation?

2.13 Show notes and transcripts

- Why are show notes and transcripts useful for you and also for your audience?

- How will you generate your show notes and/or transcript?

- What kinds of images will you include in your show notes?

2.14 Collaboration and freelancers

- What are the pros and cons of co-hosting a podcast?

- If you are considering co-hosting, write down what you would bring to the arrangement and what skills you would need in a co-host. How will you make this work for the long term?

- How could you use freelancers to make podcasting easier? What tasks could you outsource?

- If you're interested in a podcast collective, what are the benefits and the things to watch out for?

2.15 Podcast workflow and tools

- What might your podcast workflow look like?

- How can you make the time to achieve this on a regular basis or how can you budget for freelance help?

2.16 How to launch a podcast

- What do you need to prepare in advance of your launch date?

- Have you decided on your launch date? Will you have time to get everything done by then?

- Do you have a content and production schedule, so you know when everything needs to be done? Does this also stretch into the weeks after launch, when you will need to post regular content to gain traction?

- Is your website optimized for possible traffic and email signups?

- Have you created your marketing material?

- How will you measure a successful launch?

2.17 How to market a podcast

- How will you market your podcast? What ideas resonate with you?

2.18 Re-purpose your podcast content

- What are some ways that you could re-purpose your podcast content?

2.19 The money side of podcasting

- What do you want to achieve with your podcast? What will make it worthwhile even if you don't make any money?

- Do you want to be an independent podcaster or work within a network where they control content and advertising?

- What are some ways you could monetize immediately?

- How could you monetize in the future if your listenership grows?

- If you want to do corporate advertising, what are some of the companies that might be interested in your niche? How will you approach them?

- How could you offer value to a community on Patreon? What might you offer for reward levels?

- Have you considered the P&L of your podcast? How will the timing of cash flow affect your business?

3.2 Speech to text: Dictation

- Why might you consider dictation? How might it help your writing?

- What's stopping you from dictating? How can you work through those issues in order to try it?

- What method of dictation might work for you?

- What tools do you need to get started?

3.3 Text to speech

- Are there any situations where you might find text-to-speech applications useful?

3.4 Voice assistants, smart speakers and devices

- In what situations have you experienced or observed people interacting with voice assistants?

- Consider what might be possible. Then go check whether it already exists.

3.5 Optimizing for voice

- Are your books available in audio on every voice ecosystem?

- Are you creating free audio content like podcast episodes or interviews for marketing?

- How can someone who chooses voice-first find you?

3.6 Artificial Intelligence (AI) and the future of voice

- What are you excited about in terms of potential for future voice technology? How can you take advantage of what might come?

- What concerns you? How might you position yourself to participate in the conversation and protect your lifestyle in the years ahead?

- How will you stay up to date with the changes in voice technology?

About Joanna Penn

Joanna Penn, writing as J.F.Penn, is an award-nominated, New York Times and USA Today bestselling author of thrillers and dark fantasy, as well as writing inspirational non-fiction for authors.

She is an international professional speaker, podcaster, and award-winning entrepreneur. She lives in Bath, England with her husband and enjoys a nice G&T.

Joanna's award-winning site for writers, TheCreativePenn.com, helps people to write, publish and market their books through articles, audio, video and online products as well as live workshops.

Love thrillers? www.JFPenn.com

Love travel? www.BooksAndTravel.page

Connect with Joanna
www.TheCreativePenn.com
joanna@TheCreativePenn.com

www.twitter.com/thecreativepenn
www.facebook.com/TheCreativePenn
www.Instagram.com/jfpennauthor
www.youtube.com/thecreativepenn

More Books And Courses From Joanna Penn

Non-Fiction Books for Authors

How to Write Non-Fiction

How to Market a Book

How to Make a Living with your Writing

Productivity for Authors

Business for Authors

The Healthy Writer

Successful Self-Publishing

Co-writing a Book

Public Speaking for Authors,
Creatives and Other Introverts

Career Change

www.TheCreativePenn.com/books

Courses for authors

How to Write a Novel:
From Idea to First Draft to Finished Manuscript

How to Write Non-Fiction:
Turn your Knowledge into Words

Productivity for Authors

Content Marketing for Fiction Authors

www.TheCreativePenn.com/courses

Thriller novels as J.F.Penn

The ARKANE supernatural thriller series:

Stone of Fire #1
Crypt of Bone #2
Ark of Blood #3
One Day In Budapest #4
Day of the Vikings #5
Gates of Hell #6
One Day in New York #7
Destroyer of Worlds #8
End of Days #9
Valley of Dry Bones #10

If you like **crime thrillers with an edge of the supernatural**, join Detective Jamie Brooke and museum researcher Blake Daniel, in the London Crime Thriller trilogy:

Desecration #1
Delirium #2
Deviance #3

The Mapwalker dark fantasy series

Map of Shadows #1
Map of Plagues #2
Map of the Impossible #3

Risen Gods

American Demon Hunters: Sacrifice

A Thousand Fiendish Angels:
Short stories based on Dante's Inferno

The Dark Queen:
An Underwater Archaeology Short Story

More books coming soon.

You can sign up to be notified of new releases, giveaways
and pre-release specials - plus, get a free book!

www.JFPenn.com/free

Acknowledgments

Thanks to my proofreader, Liz Dexter at LibroEditing, and to my beta readers: Alexandra Amor, Jules Horne, and Orna Ross for their useful comments.

Thanks to Jane Dixon Smith at JD Smith Design for the cover, my business logos and both podcast logos.

Thanks to Dan Van Werkhoven and Alexandra Amor for their help with the podcasts every week.

Thanks to my podcasting friends who contributed quotes to the book: Mark McGuinness, Lindsay Buroker, Mark Leslie Lefebvre, J Thorn, Rachael Herron, Barry Pearman, Jeff Adams and Will Knauss.

Thanks also to Lisa M Lilly and Christoffer Petersen for allowing me to use their pitch emails.

Lightning Source UK Ltd.
Milton Keynes UK
UKHW020335060620
364543UK00017B/1121